a world away

a world away

Gordon Greenall

First Published 2013

Editing and proofreading: Maureen Morris

Published by Gordon Greenall Associates
4 Park Road, Chipping Campden, Gloucestershire, GL55 6EA

Printed and bound in England by The Dorset Press, Dorchester

ISBN 978-0-9565242-1-8

Contents

A World Away

An orphan child looked back
At the house she'd never seen –
But the painting made it plain
That all memory of this place
Had occurred within a dream

Once a place of simple Games –
Such as flying brown paper kites
Has been superseded now by
Forms in midget mega bites –
And iPods playing giga bites

Where – she wondered – did life
Go wrong – what changed from
Traditional music and merry song –
From cycle rides in empty streets
To trees climbed – as daring feats

Where have dream's wonder gone
That once went to bed in a song
Rocking us into a Bo Peep sleep
While counting gamboling sheep
Till all of us – are rhymed with Orpheus

Let her thoughts be preserved
In a form that can easily be served –
Taken into avid minds from screens
Via eyes that have never first hand seen
Games played in near empty lanes
And (must needs mown) village greens

So – let all children look back
At a life they have never seen –
But painted so to make it plain
That all memories of this place
Were once so real – but now are only dreams

Bowels Aflame

A prescription waits for the sickly man –
Brought on by bowels aflame
As cruelty misbehaves as only cruelty can –
Mocking a man in chronic pain
So the torture – nature planned has cut deep
Into a soul that bled and now starts to seep

The puss of ill-informed – ill-sent tumours –
Hard and hot on sore infected skin
Worn over neck and face and throbbing soars
Well advised to not let puss matter in
But if they weep – quickly lance their head
And squeeze till those antagonists have fled

The subject of vigilance and sterile dressings
Used to sooth disabling distressings –
As they batter sore matter with a hale storm
Clattering – swirling as a Maelstrom
Of darting – dashing cells bent on body crime
Till thwarted by good reason – sense and time

Time to send for those cleansing purgatives –
Such medication called upon to gain
Recompense with antidotes and curatives –
To treat this vicissitudenous dull pain –
While cruelty misbehaves to mock the man
With such chronic pain – as only cruelty can –
Still unthwarted by such purgatives as lime
Good reason – sense and time

Grey Monoliths

Broad monuments surround me now
Proffering their curt good days
While absorbing empty praise –
For I am down among
The darkest hours
Where no birds sing
And there are no flowers.

Grey concrete – creaking monoliths
Force their way – fore and aft
Like intergalactic craft
From an ashen desert
Of raw concrete –
Where no birds sing
And flora is fast in dark retreat.

This wasteland has my germinating thoughts
Where their seeds are blown around
To land on stony ground –
Set on by a charcoal storm
Of treacle paint –
Where no birds sing –
Choked on ligatures of restraint.

Blackened dreams swarm over me
Contemplating Luciferian arts –
Misconstrued – torn apart –
Drowning in cold sweat –
Bolt upright, awake –
Where no birds sing –
All drowned in a phosphor lake.

Filled with drugs – well prescribed
To clear the throbbing brain –
Dull each ache and pain –
For I am down among
The darkest hours
Where no birds sing
And there are no flowers.

A Socialist Democracy

While believing in our socialist democracy
It is not what you do – more what you say
That deals in the truth and is free of hypocrisy
There is no need for outdated autocracy
If to our communist rules all are let play
While believing in our socialist democracy

So let us banish all forms of plutocracy
And punish those who don't do it our way
That deals in the truth and is free of hypocrisy

For as a leader I know it's not what we see
But faith shown in us at the end of the day
While believing in our socialist democracy

Anyone wanting to keep clear of controversy
Must be out parading on the first day of May
That deals in the truth and is free of hypocrisy

We will re-educate all those who dare disagree –
Those non-believers we've been holding at bay
While believing in our socialist democracy
That deals in the truth and is free of hypocrisy

Barbaric Leering Rings

This bull ring – a cruel place to battle –
A crude – 'crowd encrusted' rotunda –
A place for un-dignifying blunders
Done to the offspring of ebonized cattle –
To let cheers go up to mask the screams –
Not bovine – but shrieked by doubters
As they cry – while trying to dream
Away – the need for blood lust – stouter

Than the truth – that such lust cruelly stains
The dust of Spain's barbaric leering rings
Such is the crude assembly that brings
Anthropomorphism to ingrate brains
They should be abolished and re-born
As somewhere useful – an arboretum
Where bolero dancers no more than strum
Flamenco guitars – beneath the stars
Where kindness and common sense have won

St Peter

St Peter – (lowered from the cross)
Called victory – though in a dead state
For he had done – with just small loss –
His duty – as a man without hate –

"See my words scatter over the day –
Catch some – catch them well –
Listen hard – hark to what words say
Answer their call and ring their bell"
For words and meanings – once freed
From their swathes of foetus flesh – leave
The earth – are astral bound for need
Of space to articulate – all that they believe

There – on high – I spy St Peter – alive –
What game is this I cry – "Bliss"
Is St Peter's gay reply – "If you strive –
You can find heights equal to this"

"For I am the words that cascaded
Down from the live husk of my cross –
And floated in fresh air – invaded
Those in need of worship free of dross."

So don't cry for me – my words are free
And can not be crucified – live
They are in thought and speech – so be
The apostle to those who thrive

And pray these words are born
To be a church – not of straw or brick
But wise words – rendering scorn –
Outcast as one more shabby trick

So use words – build a nave where ever you stand
Furnish the altar with a wave of your hand
Call all those bathed in the teachings on sea or land
Join in their joy – just as St. Peter had planned

Baked Beans And A Bike

My sow's got swine fever –
If I'm to believe her
And can't snort a note
From her nose to the back of her throat –
Just as the cat lost her way
And the cry of her anthem comes
As a sharp meow – with a Tom
In a bed of pelargoniums.

So – off such a backdrop
I wonder if my cat and my sow
Can put their troubles aside
And get together some how –
In a meeting of minds –
Twined with impunity –
Like so many of us here –
Within a European Community.

Such unity would be great – for when I'm dead
So I've read – I'll be heaven fed
Taken up on a cloud
Directly from my feather bed.
When I arrive –
(As long as I am let in)
I'll be pampered by serifs and nymphs
Serving whisky, brandy and gin.

A place without trouble and strife
For all spiritual life
And where every girl is a blonde –
Who fatally falls for my wand
And my sow's swine fever
Is cured now and forever –
And there's no need for mittens –
Or cats with kittens.

For breakfast I'll have
Beans on fresh buttered toast –
Followed by a glance of the papers
Then before my full Sunday roast –
I'll put on my cycling clips
And ride – well – as far as I like –
Cos in heaven – a man can travel miles –
On baked beans – and a 'bike.

Mandeep Jo And Jacqueline

How well they lookout for me –
Rush about for me
Tend to my failings
Put up with my railings

Set me on a healthy course –
Cross check and endorse
A treatment plan –
That makes me what I am

All skilled girls and beauty too
Without them – I know not
What I'd do – but I know –
To say it – is fair –
I am much better for their care

So I am brought to believe
That I – or any man –
Would surely win
When in the care – of
Mandeep – Jo and Jacqueline

Sean

26th April 1954 to 26th October 2009

An Irish man departed
This earth today –
Not long enough
From his birth –
Gone in too much haste
For my taste

I would like to know
Why my son – my brother
My mate – had to leave
At such a rate –
For he truly was son –
Brother and mate

Bluebells

An under-cloak of porcelain bells
Thought of as the woodland swells –
With need of those lace canopied days
That let through Springs spun rays
To bath these coppiced spreads
Of bowed and bobbing heads –
In a light that filters true
And paints them rare – a Wedgwood blue.

The winter frosted swirls of dust
Are lain – damp to bed in trust
Of a springly radiance of fashion –
Worn courtly – as an overcoat of passion
Kissed by bees – flitting weightless ghosts –
Pollen spreading navvies – seeking hosts –
Their Queenly circles adding to the mix
Of towering trees and sapling sticks.

Reaching columns of dark
Purple and grey-brown – raspish bark
Wrapped around the beech and larch –
Supporting infant green and sun glazed arch
By random search – where buds abound –
To burst as a verdant roundelled crown
Atop the under-cloak of porcelain bells –
Who really are the woodland's swells.

That Wet Summer

The worst on record for many years
Grey corn – germinating (green) within the ears –
Standing as a backdrop
To (ever swelling) harvest fears –
With only old men cursing
About those sodden times
When Young buzzards were seen rehearsing
Their acrobatic swoops and lunges
To dive – in death delivery plunges.

No pollinating bees in flight
Only late – the unseen sight
Of the barn owl leaving perch
In search of shrews and other morsel dues –
With occasional screech
Punctuating the broking night –
Far from sight – in unnoticed flight
Returning with vole – devoured
High in dust laden rafters –
A one course repast – without afters.

Few flocks of starlings
Peppering the evening skies
Now (with storm) obliterating
Already muffled cries –
Muted by a torrent – washing out
Bee dwellers paper hives –
And a failing harvest that strives
To avoid a plague of par boiled mash –
Still sat in a million skins –
Instead of rounded gathering bins.

That wet summer stole the harvest
From those – doing their best
As growers – keen among the showers
In their gathering quest
Of all abundance – while the swallows
Left for baking ovens south –
While northern latitudes missed out
Due to wet – still uncut arrears
As echoing granaries resound
To lack of sound – the worst for many years

Arctic Brawlers

I feel the autumn fall
As it comes to call –
Turning summer graze
Into a Khaki Crystal maze
Once deserted by the fading mistral haze –
Grass drained of all nutrition
Forced into a 'winter time' attrition.

Now caught in shafts
Of October blasts –
So keen they seem
Intent on cutting life in half –
As tinder grass dances
To the rutting chorus laugh
Of the barking red deer buck –
Immersed in cervid rut.

Migration takes her toll
On summer callers –
Making way for Arctic
Webbed-feet brawlers –
Come to dwell and over winter
In wet land marsh – well below
Harsh month-long nights –
To roost on softer snow.

Arriving as they do – bedraggled –
These unruly northern Gaggles
Seem intent – at least
On permanent breaches of the peace –
Necks stretched – wings akimbo
Seemingly unable to find a restful limbo –
As their ill thought quarrels
Appear born of pugilism –
Not bound (are they) by courtly morals.

The sun will dip far below the edge
Before returning north once more
On the feast of St. Thomas
As the earthly tilt swings – as done before –
To bring about the rustlings
Of snouted – once sleeping inquisitors
And cause the squawking geese to leave –
Giving sway to a wing of –
More amenable sub-saharan visitors.

Another Waiting Room

Yet another waiting room
Done out in mauve and gloom –
Where twenty folk sit captured
In orthopaedics and fractures –
My arrival adds one more
To the baleful score
As I'm told – sit over there –
If only you can find a chair.

The low hubbub turns to a shout
As I hear my name called out
And I'm ushered to an inner room
That smells of – well – impending doom –
Though very clean
Marks of pain can still be seen
As the nurse – so prim and neat
Urges me – to take a seat.

I'm in a room with just a chair
And bed – with nothing more in there.
The ceiling and walls are brilliant white
Lit by a bright fluorescent light –
All walls are fitted with notices and towels
And many dispensers of soap
A computer screen flashes all –
Save for even a little hope.

The inner sanctum is curtained off
But voices from behind the screen –
As well as drawers and doors are heard
Though none are seen –
I hear many footsteps to and fro
From shoes that mutter wear and tear –
I lean forward in my solitary chair
Stare below the curtain –
To a floor that's echoes of despair.

Finally the specialist emerges
Like an actor taking to the stage –
To vigorously shake my hand
And claim my fears he will assuage –
For the damage is beyond an operation –
So the good news is – I won't see him again.
But to fear not – for he will pass me on
To clinicians – who specialise in pain.

The Picking Boys

As a boy I was fed and watered
Summer quartered –
In a patchwork quilt of fields –
Put there to gather harvest yields –
Picking beans and half pots of peas
And then sent aloft to tops of trees
In search of egg and Victoria plums –
Plucked by nimble fingers and thumbs.

Cocooned in four miles square –
My determined boyhood ended there –
Amid twelve pound chips
Two filled – for only one and six –
A week's work for fair words and dues
Enough for new school shoes –
Socks and a shirt or two
So needy – they were overdue.

Waltzing baskets snaking to and fro
Between lunch and tea and every row
Of trees – stood like large green sheep
Till sheared of fruit and the need to creak –
Baskets of flasks filled with milky tea –
Sandwiches decked with wasp or bee –
All scoffed and quaffed and then
Back aloft to the pickings once again.

Boys prepared to run the ladders
Each one swift – each one madder
Than the growers shout –
As baskets dropped round about
His shins and balding head –
Though none took heed of what was said –
For boys turned into men
Right there – in that idyll –
Oh how I wish – I was there still.

A Beach Peach Disaster

Down on the beach – while eating a peach –
I saw a message in a bottle coming into reach –
The brittle bottle brushed against my leg – but
Being broken – it put a cut on my foot –
I asked the lifeguard if he new any first aid
He replied, "No – but I now a young nursery maid."
A very friendly girl, he praised, whom he'd met
On a Sunday morning church parade –
And then they wiled away the rest of the day –
As together they played in a small woodland glade –

I told him straight that I wasn't in any state
To show interest in his woodland date
For neither his maid – her parade nor their glade
Could administer first aid –
I then tried to persuade this beach renegade
To take care of my foot repair –
But he insisted I go to A&E and get my foot care there.

I sat in a deck chair which broke –
Letting me down to the ground – enhancing
My (care and repair) despair.

Finally now on my own – completely alone –
I got through – via the loan of a blackberry phone –
To ambulance control – where I was told
To wait at the harbour gate
Because the ambulances were all running late –
Attending to several maids
Superficially injured in a beach Leech raid
On a church parade and who had then all ending up
In a small woodland glade.

So I borrowed bandage and plaster –
And became master of my own – cut foot disaster.

Something Borrowed

Funeral dress would be less
Formal without a black tie –
An item many men have borrowed
From me – rather than buy –
So it seems clear in the depths of sorrow
People are still prepared to borrow

In this age of plenty – borrowing
Seems at least as rife as when strife
Was the order of the day – when
Long hours were worked for little pay –
That's how it was – as my granddad swore –
There was a universal dearth
All through the Second World War
Bicycles as rare as icicles

In mid-June – Granddad would croon –
Taken in 'that' way, you might say –
With no thought for the new pedestrian –
His redundant cycle clips – chapped lips
Or even shoe leather – during inclement weather

Vegetables were treated like royalty
Cabbages were January Kings –
With the little or nothing – winter brings
There was a lack of vegetables to rack –
That time when chitlings often went missing
"And missing chitlings never came back" –
Granddad would say – as Grandma
Called "'ere mind your back."
While taking logs from the stack
To keep the fire in – so Granddad
Would not catch cold – during his long reminiscing

This reminiscing reminds me –
I borrowed my Mates second missus
Way back in the sixties –
She's now gone long in the teeth –
Talks of nothing but grief –
Each time her ex-husband and I meet
He says, "Thanks! What you did was such a relief"
So be careful what you borrow –
While times are slack –
Cos there are some things –
Once acquired – you can never give back

Queues

Queues long
Queues short
All are fraught

Carolyn

She came – as one of us –
To work – without fuss –
Notes balanced on knees –
Discreetly sat –
Completely at her ease
Helpfully observing –
Never self serving

Self effacing – self driven
In her search for news
Of Bourton on the Hill –
With such professionalism –
It was a joy to hear her
Calling characters to appear
About their business –
Coarsely or with finesse
At the heart of their doings –
Their playings – their wooings
Which she selflessly recorded
As dues accorded

A world of infinite time
Seasons resplendent –
Memories sublime –
Fitting in with their
Uppings and downings –
(Anywhere else they'd
Be toings and froings)
As she captured
And committed to page
Their confoundings –
Their oneness with
Idyllic surroundings

She was the wordsmith's key
That unlocked a community
Combing out the layers –
Defining the players –
Behind her columbine mask –
Her self defining – old writing task

Expendable Men

Though broken were young men by war
Wounded in the dark and distant past –
Now (luckily) fewer than they were before

As myopic politicians and generals swore
That peace (when come) would last
Though broken were young men by war

As peace comes with blood and gore
Casualty numbers (that were) once so vast
Now (luckily) fewer than they were before

Those safe at home all call out for more
Killing of foreign sailors at the mast
Though broken were young men by war

All those heroes who died by the score
Will have medals posthumously cast
Now (luckily) fewer than they were before

All those casualties who – wars deplore
Might recover from that cruel hell's blast
Though broken were young men by war –
Now (luckily) fewer than they were before

Called To Fly

They were a special litter –
That glitter of butterflies –
Who danced before my eyes –
Were they from my past? I asked –
For today's butterflies seem rather shy
As though called to heaven –
Called to fly –
Pupated – before being freed to die

Where is the regal Monarch – late
Purple Emperor – or maybe
The Empress Cleopatra – or great
Queen of Spain's Painted Lady

The Duke of Burgundy – has his
Red admiral – skippers gone to sea
His brown shoemaker – Apollo –
Swallowtail – Weavers Fritillary
Sooty Copper – all are proper

But stripped of their glitter
They all are frittered away
As though called to heaven –
Called to fly
Pupated – before being freed to die

The Emerald Moon

In Memory of Sean O'Reilly

The emerald moon stayed rising
Along dusk's dark horizon –
Chasing hard the morning light
From the lateness of the night –
Weighed down by crystal spangles –
Dumbing down the tangles
Of blackthorn and the haw –
Both held prisoner till the thaw

Where the dawn light lingered
At the fulcrum of the day
Be-sponged by a bleak dull gray
Canopy – of (colourlessness) held spray –
Low above those irregulars
Who came here – especially to pray
To the blessed fruits of the virgin
And our brother – death has drawn away

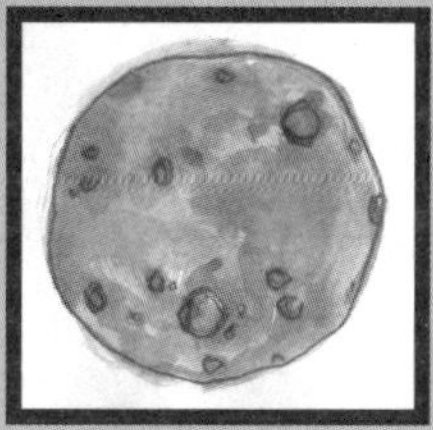

The emerald moon bore witness
To this somber – uniform of lowering –
Done in respect of this former alter boy
Who filled us all with so much joy –
And the saddest moment of the day –
Was when the mourners
Turned from the grave –
And slowly walked away

Where the emerald moon – stood mottled
By the bottom of a Black Bush bottle –
Drained in a toast to our brother
At the saddest moment of the day –
Which was when the mourners
Turned from the grave –
And slowly walked away.

Did I Let You Down

A Memory of Molly

Molly – Did I let you down some how?
I think not – hope not –
You were so gentle – so deliberate –
So delicately game – unbowed
While I was born a couple of paces
From the plough

But I feel we were the same
Some how – overshadowed –
Ill considered – hindered –
Though clean of air – Nordic by affairs –
Come from afar –

Not to be taken by magic carpet –
Let – quite unfit –
Into a desert viper pit –
An unctuous Arabian bazaar –
Sepid though we are
of skin – of consience and of kin

Both inspired by the peal
Of multi coloured penstemon bells
South ripening fruit –
Lakeland tors and fells –
Woodland trails and quenching wells

Going with the quiet of boots
On fresh fallen snow –
Lit by lime light – at middle night –
From a full moon glow –
Fond of the laden holly bough –
Or dancing flames – of cherry log
Calling us in – away from the chill
Of a late November's fog

Both drawn – I'm sure –
Not too late –
To take up paper
And with pen create
A self evoking
thought provoking 'word estate'

Note:

Sepid in Persian Poetry means white. Nordic by affairs in this context means a) Fresh or clear of air – good – bracing b) Clear unpolluted: therefore better visibility helping to see things more clearly c) Large open place easier to move around. Not clogged with waste products: unhindering

Stained In Glass

I looked up to a group of men
Their movement was of then –
A time long past – far in retreat
Their sandalled feet baring – indiscreet
Marchers – striding to a silent horn
Signalling a Christian dawn
Where all were simply clad as was the lad
Who hurriedly scurried after them

Into the bright flats and folds
Lit in countless greens and golds –
In buttercup – barley and plum –
Strident in a variety of blues –
With purple and violet hues
And brick and tile shades
Caught in light – as that of flame
And sombre greys of metal frame

Where these new adherents –
With net and crook variants –
Have taken up the cause
Of spreading the word of their lord
Around graze – lake and arables
Who's teachings were spread as parables
Depicted in crafted glass of sand and red
Bonded in soldered patchways of lead

Patterned over flint-stone floor
Dull stone walls – brass inlays – more
By the rainbow sunlight veils
Spread as drapes over alter rails –
Enhanced with the seraphim's fiery glow –
Virtue's and cherubim flow
From the cavorting blaze
So swiftly turned to a dancing glaze

Their simple lives emboldened –
By 'He' to whom they were beholdened –
Told in melted silica and tone – shed
Where-ever sun's rays bled
Over floor or overhead – strident –
Solar lit through vibrant glaze
Showing how their history came to pass –
Framed and stained in glass

Civilization At Bay

The Standing wheat waved seductively
On an inland breeze – that ran
Across the piece – through punctuated
Gaps opened through the span
Of greening hedge and broad-leaf trees

More – those older men drew my mind
Towards the wonders of nature –
Populated hedgerows with sharp spines
Homing a concubine of creatures
Each tends the other with bold nurture

As they worked passionately to provide
For a skulk of young foxes –
A dray of rabbits – et in a day of habits
And sable stoat cubs besides
Wild bees making honey in wax boxes

From nectar given up by wild flowers
Such as those hips and haws
And blackthorn buds opened all hours
To pollinate – with the leg hairs
Of insects from stamen to it's stigmas

Though this rustic idyll shadowed still
By rancour and course ill will
From baying dogs in a manic pursuit
Of Reynard – as bugled brutes
Called them on through standing corn

To a bloody scene of red vixen torture –
And debauched inbred dogs –
With so short a time for chasing tails
Urged on with whips that flog
Those who fail – sure to take the flail

At a gin trapped vixens sickening cry
For freedom – let go cruelly on
Until the pack are availed upon to try
And carry out a piteous liaison
Orchestrated by death of a fox at bay

As standing corn waves seductively
On an inland breeze – blowing
Westerly over lees now productively
Grazing new spring born lambs
Six fields away – peacefully growing

A Swathe Of Greensward

A tall ash tree scattered over me
Her flying seeds – colloquially mouthed as 'keys'
Flaying and gliding – pitching – yawing
Searching for mulch – as seeds reforming
Had to – in their own way – twisted and spiralled –
Catching the late spring gusts – all rivalled
One by the other – at first swarming –
Finding mulch for root and spawning –

So below – the grass of liquid greens –
Which seem to flow by germinated means –
Starting short – growing tall
Against the woodland's darkening wall
Of olive – kelly and holly – emerald
And agate – all as in a spate of 'paint'
For freshening spring – with Aquamarine
Turquoise – moss and – Chartreuse

Such a patchwork of greens it seems
Is a never ending collage of dreams –
Only limited by the imagination –
A mind of greens recalled from germination
Of thoughts – vaunted vegetable-like
As greens remembered – eat them up –
Liquidize but don't despise them –
Masticise them – plucked straight from the stem

So all is green – as the countryside screen
Is rolled out – it's whereabouts
Never much in doubt – for the meadows
Grazing fields – orchards and lees
Re-grass to feed the beasts that pass
All this green vegetation is a part of life –
It's photosynthesis leaves us in a state of bliss
As it takes in – (intra-leaf) – greenhouse glare
Returned to us as their re-invigorated air

So we decorate our parks – our public places
Vertical green walls with elevated bases
Of well watered root – called upon to shoot –
To foliate – to blossom in a water sate –
And in doing – plant a concrete forest – green
Urbanising – suburbanising – placated
Primates can now stretch for greensward
Without the need to be – re-located

Bell Ringing

My lucidity of wit
Was disturbed many times –
Being numbed by a validity of chimes –
From the school bell – whether rung poorly
Or whether run well

I believe the bell
And the paucity of teaching
Were – together – very far reaching –
Where – I can't tell – or whether done poorly
Or whether done well

In my poor mind –
Often vilified then accused
By those claiming not much amused –
By the school bell – whether rung poorly
Or whether rung well

So mal-adroitness
Has now been diagnosed –
By experts – expertise presupposed –
From a university spell – whether done poorly
Or whether done well

Their pomposity
Is from a scarcity of ideas –
Never confronted by irksome fears
From a reality spell – whether done poorly
Or whether done well

So justly qualified
They all send me down –
With out tears – smile or – a frown
From the just bell – whether rung poorly
Or whether rung well

Views said of me
That could never be fair
As many observers hadn't been there
From the school bell –whether rung poorly
Or whether rung well

Now prayers said
Are said for me a good
Man and godly – who never would –
In a lifetime of achievement ring the bell poorly
Only ring the bell well

Wrong Place

I met cousin Alf last Michaelmas day
Carrying a box of discovery seeds –
Which he must plant without further delay –
He had bought them from a woman in tweeds
But they grew into such a poor array –
In an unwanted – display of weeds –
He moaned, "I've been sold a pup in a sack
So I'll demand she pays my money back."

"Look 'ear Misses these seed're no good." He moaned
"They never grew into what I'd expected."
"They were all that I'd claimed." She then groaned
From the name 'discovery' you should've suspected –
And if you weren't sure you could have phoned –
Then I'd have explained what you had collected
So – you're wrong young man it's not a disgrace
Weed's are just plants growing in the wrong place

"You see discovery means a surprise
So those you purchased were always a gamble
I was not taking you for a prise
Fool – you should've known by my opening ramble –
For I'd not try to take out of you – a rise –
After having heard your sad preamble
I'm, of the opinion you're not worth salt
So – I won't claim that it's entirely your fault"

"May I suggest though – you crop the first row
Of those nettles with long pointed leaves
Which when dry can be rolled – then smoked as blow –
But be careful of those plant cutting thieves –
You will know them by their pallid grey glow
So make sure all that you grow – you retrieve –
For the crop you've grown aids medicinal recovery –
That's why – some call it a 'miracle' discovery

Coded Wooing

I planned on telepathy
To break down her apathy
Towards me and my future
As her most admirable suitor –
At first my plan worked quite well
I know – I could tell
That she was justly impressed –
Though she kept her desires – well suppressed.

I sat opposite her whenever I could
With the knowledge it was doing her good –
Being bombarded with positive waves
As she braves
All that – inane patter
Known as female chatter –
When (I know) she'd rather be –
Somewhere else – alone with me.

There was though – a glitch
Well – more of a hitch –
For I was in difficulty
With my mastery of telepathy –
Each day I would correspond
With this girl – of whom I was fond –
But no matter how hard I tried –
She never once replied.

I went back to my English teacher
And said "I'm unable to reach her –
Though I've done all that you've said –
Even emptied my head
Of other attractions –
In fact all further distractions
That might explain the distinct equivocation
In her one and only communication.

She thought for a while
And then consulted a pile
Of miscellaneous notes
Written as a series of quotes –
Then – shrieking in despair –
She pulls out some of her hair
As she finally howls,
"You need to do more work on your vowels."

I was not very impressed
In fact I was more than a little depressed –
For this was the very device
She'd used before – when I'd sought her advice –
For then – to my consternation –
The problem was with my punctuation
And to add more to my despair
My consonants were – again judged only – fair.

I showed her my beloveds note
In which she had wrote
That my skin was too light
And I'm not the right height –
My personality's not great
And she could never date
A man who can't dance –
At this point I had to ask, "Do you think
I'm still – in with a chance?"

My teacher decidedly winced
And then positively flinched
As she shook her head
And then said,
"I must give you your account –
It's made out for the full – and final amount.
And as you've so miserably failed this course –
May I suggest – that in future – you try contact by Morse."

Scrapped

I was proud of the way
That some of the crowd – they
Were happy to part
And make room for my donkey and cart –
I had been asked – between rides – to
Collect the manure and 'do
Whatever one does with it, from the street –
And – dear boy remember –
What ever you do –
For heavens sake – do always be discreet' –

It was the same each year
I was always asked to clear
Away this or that – take it (in a sack)
And dump it in an anonymous stack –
Behind somewhere or other –
It didn't matter as long as it was of no bother –
Behind the scout hut –
Was where I left half a ton of soot –
That caused some consternation
When the hut went up
The soot adding greatly to the conflagration

One year when scrap metal gathering
I caused holy lathering –
When on the pile of scrap and the like –
I'd inadvertently stacked the vicar's old bike
So it was with some relief
When I came to grief
And was persuaded that it was time make way
For a new scrap horse and dray –
Though I refused to part
With my old pals – my donkey and cart

Fragmented Snow

The buds by now are split and spread
As are the dreams inside my head –
They to seed and set and grow –
My dreams to fragment and snow
In showers of bleak delight
To haunt me through the blackest night.

Seeds need rich soil and warmth –
From the sweat of summer earth –
As my dreams need sleep
That's settled – long and deep –
Not a fitful nightly spread
Of black demons – loose inside my head.

Let me sleep in climbing spring
And high summer – beyond the ring
Of whit bells and pageant spells
So – when provoked to wake –
I spill into days that no longer bake
My arid brain – in need of rain
To drown my recurring dread
And flush those demons
From my throbbing head.

Rejoicing

At the voicing
Of another death –
Life in decline
Who's? Not mine

Cruise V Shoes

In this world where the streets
Are scarred with lines of cars
Waiting as they do for the
Occupant to press the electric
Start and create a spark
Of (cylinder capacity) Piston activity

As do people – labelled throng –
Come along making their own
Journey – either short or long –
Simply – slowly – these lowly
Travellers – maybe bare of foot
But must make rest in trust

That these streets will separate
The settled from the metalled –
One being fettled of sole
And the other settled of fuel
Ready for the highway duel –
Man and machine with different
Needs and different speeds

Caught in fully armed action –
One with loudly clanking claxon
While the other puts on banter –
Finding speed hard – once at a canter –
No contest calls the metal man
"We have cleared the way
For lorries cars and omnibuses.
While those pedestrians were
Given a whacking before we sent
Them packing" He cusses.

But justice puts her fingers in
And decides she will punish him
For foul – course metallic attack –
On the whole pedestrian pack –
So – bringing in endorsements
For those who drive without due care
While ordering those same drivers – that
With pedestrians – they must share
The highways and byways which
Promise travellers going everywhere –
But often – in obverse contrast –
Going nowhere – fast

The Lucky Ones

It was those long hours of waiting
That always left us shaken –
Stood to attention in mud
And blood and things we couldn't mention
Until the cannons roar
And good men are taken by the dogs of war

Choked on cordite – lost in bad light
Asthmatics of the mustard gas attack
As we are freed like homing pigeons
To return to the (never ending) fight
Devised by generals and international spite

Brave lads drawn to write – between
The censers pencil lines – about their plight
If my good luck changes
And I am to become a casualty
Please think well of me
Divested of my youthful strength –
Gone without fanfares and flares –
Only salvoes of threadbare nonsense
Through the barbed wire and bugle fence
Sent out there – beyond medical care –
Measuring my length –
Finally drained of Earthly strength

As we the givers of our lives
Are called upon to leave our mud lined hives
And go as lions over a grim mire – churned savannah
Towards defoliated trees once manna
To a chorus of birds and a richness of bees

We the lucky ones no longer afraid of German guns
Or the yperite that chased our lunges –
One more time flex our tongues
And whistle as we ascend the rungs
That lead we 'the given'
Onto obelisks and into the arms of oblivion
Played out by the cannons roar –
Good men taken by the dogs of war

Note:
Yperite: lethal (mustard) gas

Tide Up

Small boat
Less crew
Harbours well
Hidden from
The stew
Of ocean swell

Cycling

Old Bike
Broken – thrown –
Forced to hike
More than a token
Mile from home

Blood And Poppies

Bold stands the blooming Flanders Poppy spread –
A valedictory parade – red as blood
To all lost souls now badly bowed or dead –
Left floating in a common grave of mud –
By devilish proportions – a generation
Wasted – without cause or compensation
For those exposed to harsh recrimination
Much ado and no congratulation

So lads pick up your khaki bags and sing –
And join your old pals – all long gone abroad
To fight and die for country and for king –
Give your stout hearts and souls up to the lord
For if you stay at home – by war un-kissed –
You'll never know what fun you've missed

Dougie Cooper

Dougie Cooper came amongst us
Not exactly Christ like
More a man on a motorbike –
Quietly – without fuss –
Soon drawn to machine folk –
Motorcyclists and exhaust smoke

He was such a cheerful chap
With the gift of laughter
Even after many a mishap –
Seldom heard to cuss –
Saying it always could be wus
After just another fall –
Not worth the worry after all

He was heard to say
I never raises me voice
For I've been married twice
And after all these years
Just one look at Dulc
Can quickly raise me pulse

He was a British Champion
In the trials side-car of Ron Langston –
Motor cycles were his passion –
Ridden in his own – inimitable fashion –
He generously offered lifts
To pedestrians who didn't always
Appreciate such transport gifts –
As he said, "I drops 'em off
And once they gets their breath back
They looks at me and then
Says – I'll never ride with you again."

So let's give a thought for
His family – their sadness
At his loss and their gladness
At his living and good temper –
All those stories we remember
For He will be missed by
All of them – and a great many
More – ageing motorcycle men

Rhyme And Reason

Scour my childhood
Observe the man made mess –
Take down the dreams
Of nightmares and screams –

Codify my patience
As the ice is dripped on me –
See my body shake
As pain – my person takes –

Relate to my head
Filled with ills brought on
By mindless words
Spoken meanly by absurd

Troubled holders
Of my sickening early years
Who called time –
On my reason and my rhyme

So scour my headlines
Observe the man made stress –
Take down the dreams
End all (black demon
Engendered) high pitched screams
All of which leaves me in a mess
Of illness caused distress

Drowned Ideas

Bright Ideas –drowned in fears
And washed away on a tide of tears –
Given cause to escape the salty squalls
That spat the air as darkness falls –
To catch the heavy moon asleep
And dodge darks cleaver sweep
Across the edge of sultry day –
Where nocturnal predants play.

Splayed out like fur and scale fans
Made up of rat and lizard clans –
To scurry and slither
Panic like – hither and thither –
These mobs of carnivores –
And various – veracious omnivores –
Intent on staying out of sight
While placating (each) ravenous appetite.

Ideas fed – quenched and rested
Wait patiently to be invested
In technological vigour –
Lines punctuated by black figures
Set out to explain the unexplainable –
To minds of men unable
To grasp the task
Of understanding ideas – masked.

So thoughts formed into plans
Are blown about by dissenter's fans –
Put to beggarly flight
By the darkness of the night –
So lost in those salty squalls
Blown in thoughts to doubter's outer walls
And left to fall as prey
For that nocturnal predants splay.

Ideas lost to wind and shark
Like (over turned) barks in the dark.
Their cries unheard –
Found drowned like a chocolate bird –
For want of an understanding nod
From an omnipotent God –
Those bright ideas – drowned in fears
And washed away on a tide of tears.

The Forest Path

The forest path bade me take it's way
Past the earthworks sett –
Where (at dusk) young badgers play –
It was about this time I saw a rough haired terrier
Coated in dried blood and mud of clay –
The (battered ratter) mainly feral –
Yelped come forth at your peril
For though I am mauled – I still hold sway
So I approached the canine stray

With a certain amount of caution
Feeling the need to at least gain his trust –
So I took a path – the one I felt I must –
The path the forest bade me take
Which lead me to a grave mistake –
For I was now involved with an angry dog at dusk –
Seeming to provoke him – with my human musk

Though the time of day seemed to favour me
As I took the precaution to hide behind a chestnut tree –
For dusk came in quickly with the rolling fog
To help disguise me from that (blood and patchwork) dog –
I consorted with the forest canopy asking for more light
Just as the heavy mist lifted to leave a starry night –
So I made my way to a squirrel's dray near the badger's sett
Where the dog's hunting instinct and the badgers met

An altercation of high decibels then occurred –
That was so one-sided it seemed to be absurd –
Between the mud and blooded terrier – now at bay
And the badgers who seemed keen about the fray –
So I strode along a forest path guided by the stars
To arrive at a place where I leapt a gate with seven bars
To rest on crunching grey-white grass – looking back
At the night sky of (a moonlight shaft)
Framed against bitter winter's black.

Ground Zero

Still today – that inferno of screams
Chills my subconscious dreams –
Awake in the bold light of day
Those haunted souls refuse to go away.
Trapped in striated ladders of debris
Frozen in a moments struggle to be free –
Contorted in the general trash –
Coated – in choking grey ash.

Now a place of many quiets
Each condemning that awful riot –
In the names of victims hurled
From their high rise world
By crazed transgressors
Claiming legitimacy from their predecessors –
In manic action done by demonic dissidents
Against all those scores of innocents.

Hollowed silences – each a family dream –
Show due respect – by holding back the stream –
The torrent of orphaned cries
That would drift towards the skies
At this concrete – chasmic void
A hundred deaths long by thirty wide.
Looked on by gaunt tourists and ghosts –
One group visitors the other – hosts.

Brought together in unifying sorrow
At this scene of demonic horror
Surrounded by monolithic marker posts –
Each derelict, silent, for the most
Decked in sad livery from a collection
Of now fading mementos of affection –
Placed there to mark a loved one remembered –
Father, Mother, daughter, son enembered.

As we leave the chill comes too –
Dragging the silence after us – to do
Their best to hold us in our terse regret
Lest we should dare to forget
The shame – the callousness
In lives lost and count of their distress
At this place where we stood with Ghosts –
At vigil with our spirit hosts

As the burnt ash settles about this space
To turn to grey this black disgrace.

The Mill Race Roars

The mill race roars
As water pours
Onto the paddle blades –
Before it cascades
To the waiting stream
Where waters dream –
Of once fine power
Turning in watts per hour –
While flattening wheels
Grinding corn to meals
And flour – ground
Down – sold by the pound –
Now just an empty noise
Entertaining school boys
And girls cartwheeling
In time to the squealing –
Of dried up metal joints
As the oil can anoints –
Bearings – none too soon –
On 'turning wheel' moon –
Beneath the mill race
That turns a pace –
As water pours –
Causing loud roars
As it cascades
Over waiting blades –
To end the dreams –
Of an old mill stream

Ballymena

With apologies to Thomas Hardy, and also 'thanks' too, for the inspiration gained from his poem, Donaghadee.

I have been to Ballymena
A cold grey Antrim Town – to see
The girl I once held close to me –
Who still dawns in Ballymena.
A girl I first met in a bar
On Douglas strand – not so far
Across the sea – from Ballymena.

Mary – I wrote to you there
For I know – as a lass so fair –
You entertained me – right
Through a bullet strewn night
As ordinance's flying din
Rose high – till day broke in.

That Betty – too – of Randalstown
Set me aching up and down
While Maureen McCann would sing
To the backing of the bullets ring.
Then there was Iris and Marion
Who joked right through this carry on –
While Jean McRae – as I remember
Danced beneath a starred September.

But that Maid – once I'd seen her
Who was so tender in tone from Ballymena
Like Susan – has no name for me
Keeping my being in secrecy
(For doubtless she is of that sort)
Who played my strings – without court
To a man of my demeanour –
On an errant trip to Ballymena.

Note:
Mary was (and I hope still is) a real person of whom I was once fond. A strawberry blonde with Hibernian eyes and Irish lilt, blessed then with the charm of youth.

A Mighty Mix Of Merriment

A mighty mix of merriment
And enriching sediment
Made our cider strong –
And through this elixir
Life would be the jollier
Though not lasting very long

In the breakfast I am cooking
There are no bacon rinds
Though there are lots of eggs –
Of the double-yoked kind
With magic mushroom vices
And black pudding slices
So much is readily devoured –

But is it just for lust or pleasure?
With my withering appetite
Called upon to bring to closure –
Drinking down a pint of swelly
Producing methane in my swollen belly

Dancing must be ripe – once fettled –
Implements employed once metalled
Guardian's of solstice – Sun and joy
With their baby girl and bonny boy
Crawling from crib to chamber pot
Of woven willow – with feathers shot

I am told – by bowmen – by showmen
Now – as they were once low men –
Before they had been pressured for
The mandatory marching off to war
Dreaming often of the cider jar
And the welcome of a four ale bar

Where there will be mix of merriment
Enriched by those escaping torment –
Back among the waiting swarm
Of well wishers – staid – content –
Home – where the cider mix is strong
To drink a toast to all those men
Who left and did not live too long

The Curfew Tolls

The curfew tolls the knell of parting day
So Nell (by candlelight) goes out to play –
And trips from the broken porch
When caught in the beam of a policeman's torch –
Who chides – "Out this late you break the law"
"But I am allowed" – she pleads – "for I am poor" –
"It is an 'on the spot fine' for lack of thought
My girl," He cries – "Or you will find yourself in court."

So it is that she is charged and arraigned
Urged to plead guilty to being framed –
"Nell you're found guilty of breach of curfew."
Say the magistrate, "So this is what I intend to do.
I'll put you on an 'asbo' without light –
You will patrol from eve to middle night."–
He then goes on to explain to Nell
If she sees suspicious types – she should ring her bell

Nell decides that she – without light
And left out to do what she will – over night
Might turn it to advantage – this her plight –
She could set up her own night school
For professionals of the oldest kind – to fool
Those burgers – who intend to rule
By curfew – while availing themselves
With goods from off Nell's shelves
And be so practised well with Nell –
In order that they should be well able
To toll the liberated – Libertinous bell

The Silent Street

The silence of the street
Has caught my eye –
Brought about from
The lack of traffic passing by –
Only dying echoes
From rare tattooing feet
Scar the hallowed silence
Of our hollow street.

The queues of cars –
Both parked and in their jams –
No longer snake this narrow thoroughfare
Like elongated trams,
Do not degrade the limestone
With their eroding black emissions –
Nor threaten crossing folk
With imminent collisions.

Red and ochre boards
Add (mutely) to the traffic's woes
With their dumb announcement
That this road is closed –
In monosyllabic language
They go on to say
That they are very sorry for
Any disruption – or over-long delay.

What are a few drainage holes
And scar like slotted trenches –
With their blue ribbed pipes
Laid out – like tubular set benches,
Waiting for the road-men
To connect them into a main
Forming a stretched out grid
Of under surface drains.

I pay them little mind
As I cross St Catharine's square –
Through the impromptu car park
That has sprung up there.
And as I look back
With glee – down digger lane –
I give thanks to heaven and the Council –
That the drain men came.

Turning Pale Grey

I go to bed with it – wakeup with it –
It daunts me – it haunts me –
It's never far away –
I ask it politely – if it will go lightly
But it's within me – it is me –
I know it's here to stay

It's big in me – takes my dignity –
It claims me – blames me –
For what I can not say –
It disturbs me while it curbs me
From wishes and the dishes
And going out to play

I suffer from it's ravings – cravings
As it dates me – berates me
Holds my life at bay
I have no relief – only inward grief
It deplores me – scores me –
Where? I can not say

It's vast – would have me in the past
It daunts me – vaunts me –
Always bars my way
From the party plate – the fire grate
So it chills me – spills me
Turns me pale grey

As I go to bed with it – am bled by it
Made gaunt as it taunts me –
It never goes away
I ask it politely why it's so unsightly
There within me – stinging me –
As it is holding sway

So I go to bed with it – wake with it –
It claims me – blames me –
Holds my life at bay
From the party plate – the fire grate –
It's still within me – it is me –
Turning me a pale grey

Note:
The Author feels the need to expound on how he feels, being unable to sleep as he is laden with illness and hoping it may be of help to fellow sufferers to know that they are not alone

White Cotton Flowers

As cotton wool sits like low lying cloud –
So is the purity of a white clad bride
Realized – as is the cadaver's shroud
Of calico – that wraps the corps that died –
So white's associated with such shock –
As early come the lambs – with joy – they ring –
Amongst salty bales penning in the flock –
Each adding to the high bustle of spring

Such occasions are rejoiced with flowers
As for lambs in meadows of white clovers
Rose of Sharon grown in tall round towers
Taller shows magnolia – tree of lovers –
Just married brides wearing white clematis –
Christmas greetings bade with amaryllis

English Elm

A backdrop of verdant undulation
Compliments the roadside hedges
Bursting with a profusion –
Of hip and haw
Bramble – sloe and many more
Hung as though for celebration
Along this mixed – celebrated row
Where sadly now – no elm trees grow

Much missed are those that stood –
As if sentinels of good hard wood
Guarding English verges from
Storm and wind blown surges –
Beneath skies of warning grey
Bringing rain storms to the day –

That then give way to rainbows
And main glows from swathes
Of boiling gold – waning
To mauves and ripe magentas –
Finally to relent as Tamarisk
So rinsed it is of complexion
So pale a man would be at risk

So – overcast pasture and lee –
Wait for a hail of sunlight shafts –
Free to boil the rolling fog away
Illuminating the choice fruit display –
Burst out in rich colours – tangerine –
Crimson – deep purple – navy – black
Overwhelmed by jackdaw – jay and crow
Where sadly still – no elm trees grow

Coup De Tat Of Dysentery

A world away a sort of freedom came –
With the release of a leading light
Of Burmese human rights –
The end of house arrest
For Aung San Suu Kyi is by far
The longest freedom step the strutting –
Junta bullies have made – in Myanmar
She – under house arrest in years of subjection
By the army – as have all those without protection –
While the officers held 'their own Generals' Election

She has been conditionally set free
So could it be the start of real democracy –
Or another false dawn along the Irrawaddy
For the Arakan – the Shan and Suu Kyi –
She – forced into years of solitude –
By strident military turpitude
Brought on by their ingestion of folly –
Coughing up – over 'Christian democrats'
Their spattering brand of misery –
Part of their manic coup de tat of dysentery

She now makes up for lost time –
Receiving a visit from her younger son –
Appropriately decked with visa –
This time not done just to tease her –
As so many dictatorial finesses
Have – before – I must confess
Such dictats would confuse all diplomats
And come to that – any peace envoys –
Exposed to such duplicitous a noise

Near a hundred tribes subscribe
To her – rather than the Generals' diatribe –
As she brings (a million people power) light
To the atrophied dictatorship of political night –
So in this part of the world with a catastrophic
History of south-east Asian despotocracy –
That spawned the brutal Khmer Rouge, Viet Cong
Now more benign – and chance of improving –
Over time – with Suu Kyi's political skills
Hopefully able to treat Burma's democratic ills –
Forming an administration – best by far
In freeing the peoples of Myanmar

The Few

Each early morning they flew
Risking life and limb – they – the few
Having an essential job to do

They had a nation to protect –
Dressed in flying blue and circumspect –
Nothing done simply for affect

They were brought from high education
Some from work or day long speculation –
All trained in flight and battle preparation

Apprentice sergeant pilots clad
As were public schoolboys – glad
To be a new flying warrior lad

Flung by Hurricane – the first fighting flier –
Then resplendent in Supermarine Mk 11 Spitfire
So they could fly farther – faster – higher

To fly against those like themselves
Public school Luftwaffe flying elves
Powered by Messerschmitt pistons and valves

Attacking without recrimination –
Just a Vicker's arm – prayer and trepidation
Seeking each others flight formation

Of noise and flashing fires – so surprised
Those who manoeuvred partly mesmerised
In fear of being 'cannon sodomized'

Morning calls 'shake a leg'
Leave your blanketed comfort peg
Up you go on sausage – bacon and egg

Again and again until your time has come
Again and again till your outdone
Or until the Battle of Britain's won

And so never will so many owe so much due –
To those circumspect young men who flew –
Those boys – those flyers – they – the few

Colours Arc Over

Ronny – Nigel and Sean –
Carolyn – Lesley and Rob
It's the empty spaces
Left by your leaving
That gives me cause to sob –
Soon with the skies turning dry
I clear from my eye –
Those salt tears that came littered with fears –
So I let their voices permeate
Through my willing ears –
Down from their rainbow
Seen as part of their new brain show

Each smiles, "Don't cry for me –
I'm here – don't you see."
Soft colours arc over – forever
The worst of the weather –
Each face makes a trace
In grey clouds – etched with life's grace –

Now I see them –
Soon to be amongst them –
Hearing laughter that relents
Far – into fair weather
And good common sense –
For in life all were true friends –
Through bickering and strife
They were admired – taken on with life –
Afterwards – no-one pretends –
Loosened are they from us –
Washed away with tears – but little fuss
For the truth is –
Time makes amends

In remembrance of six friends who succumbed to cancer and are all sadly missed.

The Fractious Dawn

The fractious dawn – while held waiting –
For the wild fire to be expunged –
Moved over the horizon – creating
Mayhem with the morning – plunged
Between vermillion light and salivating –
Magenta tinged storm clouds – that lunged
Towards the epicentre of the blundering
Cambium – none the better for her thundering

So fire – (combusting fuel below) seemed to stand
Firm – as well drilled lancers might – in wait
Of screaming cavalry men and horses hand
In hand – rolling like clouds of savage bait –
Bearing down on fire's firm defence of land
She claims as hers – as she sparks the beard of fate –
Lighting up his ridge and furrow – scowling brow
Felt to be Tempest's call to arms – and how

This mêlée of elements – crimson coated –
Verses purple grey and mauve – high booted
Tumble storm – damping – dancing lancer's bloated
By success of scalding gaseous blues – mooted
Favoured all the night – till dawn awoke and voted
For cousins thunderbolt and lightening – nepotism fruited
In phoney conflagration of spitting sparks – fooled
By Thor's acid juices – so wanton mayhem is cooled

As bystanders look high towards east south east
When thunder's breath douses conflagration's spite
Put to rout by Vapid's sword – wielded by the beast
Of storms – rumbling – grumbling – putting to flight
The archers of Incendiaris – as their arrows ceased
To frazzle the bulbous clowns of morning light –
Now – with hand on the epicentre of vain
Cambium – while flying the flag of morning rain

Thirty Years Past

From boyhood, fast taking flight
To adulthood and her delights.
From school, to site, to factory
Went youths, we two or three.
One, to marriage and with wife
To reproduce new born life.
But speed showed how it had lied
The day that David sadly died.

A life condensed from it's full span –
Devolved to each and every man.
Three score and ten were only bate,
Reduced to fleeting twenty eight.
Short lived, this Campden man,
Taken as his life began,
Set to take his turn with hand
To work upon the family land.

Sickening felt the awful smack
Of that random death attack,
Of those twisted, tumour cells
Invading venal, blood canals.
Laying low and making ill,
Such a man with so much will.
Losing, at such a dreadful cost,
With battle over, life was lost.

Remember him, who is not here,
Gone from us for many a year.
Not stiff, nor grey, nor bowed,
Not older than he was allowed.
Still displayed in youthful face –
Quicker he than our slow pace
Destined to live throughout eternity
Youthful as a sapling tree.

His history has not yet gone,
For those of us who linger on.
Remembering his honest strength
And his old fashioned common sense.
Ever guarded by St James,
The guardian of his last remains,
As the spirits join him now and then,
Of more and more good Campden men.

In Memory of David Hobbs

Corked Wine

With a flavour horrific
And a smell soporific –
Corked red or white wine
Can be judged only fine
For cleaning out sinks –
But surely – never to drink –

For the Bilious taste
Of this corrupted grape waste
Replaces tannins and ripe summer fruits
With the odour of navvies boots –
The reek of (week long worn) nylon socks –
And unwashed butchers smocks

An odour of athlete's foot
A bag of rotting damp soot –
For it's impossible to refine
A bottle of sour corked wine
So I'd rather drink meths
Or a quart – of distilled turpentine

'cos when wine's contaminated –
It matters not when it was dated
For it can never be sated –
And never fit to be consecrated

For when the priest wavers
When chanting – this is the blood of our saviour –
The congregation – as one – will decline
Chanting back – the Lord must be ill
Perhaps he has a chill or his fill
From this demon's (malice filled) challis –
Of secular – confessional – corked wine

The War Memorial

Standing tall – erect
As if to create an effect –
Of a soldier drawn to attention
In readiness for his last mention –
Etched into a page of lime
Dulled (like memory) by time –
Before sent to unending sleep
On (the once green) fields of Ypres.

Fields now adulterated – post dated
Obliterated – cremated
And burnt blithely off
With disregarding cough –
Into a ravenously obscene
All consuming mud machine –
Turned by bomb and shell
Into a self-defeating hell.

The 'I's' in names each shed a tear
Only when the rains appear –
As if those men in their misguided sleep
Periodically wake and weep –
To rinse the greying Bisque
Of this monumental obelisk
As do
Their unborn sons and daughters too.

Patterned – geometric –
Eight sided – octagonectic –
Presented in the round
Where named dead can be found –
A centrepiece with gabled cross
Atop a pinnacle of loss –
Decked in a livery of names
Secured in their oblongated frames.

A neat monument
Of limestone bonded in cement
Surrounded by a paving beat –
Laid out for those parading feet
That stall – (for a moment) – as they pass
On to the short clipped grass –
Not cast out to neglect –
This place – bathed in due respect.

Respect for men taken from their sleep
And their keep of 'in lamb' sheep –
Taken from the flow
And harvest of the barley mow –
Taken from the milking cow
And from behind the horse drawn plough –
From the woodland trees
And from their cousined communities.

This place where muted passion
Leaches – drizzle fashion –
On command
From holders of the black arm band
As more emotions stem
From those words – 'We shall remember them'.

Blue Or Black

The black skies have turned to blue
Now the dawn has lit the plough
That worms the earth beneath the bough –
Where David laughs from cirrus cloud
And calls aloud – for me to join him now.

But how far away is he?
Too far for my poor eyes to see –
More than three and a half leagues high
In wisplike strands across July –
Though still calling out
For me to join him there – en sky –

He has been gone so long –
My memory is weak and mist is strong –
In her is the air of a simpering breath
Calling on me to be with him in death –
As she sings her siren's song
For my life – to pass quickly on.

In my dishevelled state I look back
And call the sky as blue not black –
Again the dawn has lit the plough
That worms the earth beneath the bough
And tells me loud – I must not crack –
Though called from cloud – I must not crack.

The Lark Folds Night Away

The Lark folds night away
Allowing room for coming day
Of melodic summers dissertation
Inviting in – a full congregation
Of bird life – if only humming
To please – come and join in
The chorus and the play

By the barley field – ranked
With embryonic green Guardsmen
Pushing through the banked
Ridge and furrow fielding –
Put to seed for yielding –
Striated in the green and brown
Of early shooting –
These crops of some renown

Swallows park above the lark
In their dalliances and dancing –
Beyond the butterflies
Who mark out their airspace –
in '3D' round – much lower in the sky
Where errant insects can be found –
Flying much nearer to the ground –

Ground of insects their interests arrayed
Across the coming day – displayed
As mediator or muse – no reason to separate –
Pay dues – for nature's freight
Gratis – kempt – manicured
Green sward – of a delegation – obscured
Of single grasses – forlorn individuals
But never objurgated as lawn –
All done as the roll call of night heralds the dawn

A Rainbow Kaleidoscope

"Catch the rainbow Bill," urged Esme Lee
"Where is it? Whimsied a dreamy boating Bill
"Over there – plain for all to see."
Scolded – a by now – irritated Mistress Lee

But Bill had – in essence – drifted cloudwards
Soaring – mindly – with a tumble of swallows –
Redstarts – Swifts and many other summer birds –
Winging – singing – chanting – though no spoken words

"Come here at once and listen," Chided Cousin Lee –
"We must find water for our bathing and refreshment too."
"But I'm not thirsty and bathing's just not me."
Were the words with which – Bill chose to disagree

"You must leave your sailing cogitation
And find water." She growls with a certain irritation –
"I'll take sand for mortar mix it in with lime and water
And build a dream house free of mud and slaughter."

He went on – "A rainbow is sky's kaleidoscope
With which I have no care – nor skill to cope –
I'd much rather soar with summer birds
Join their music of sweet melodies though no spoken words

Condemned Cottages

I was sent – in my capacity as council
Inspector – to condemn a terrace of old cottages
They being a health hazard and in the way
Of the new ring road – opposed by
Temperamental environmentalists –
Concerned about daub and wattleages
Some cats – a family of bats living on the edge
And temperants wishing
They'd never signed that pious pledge

I found drunks on bunks –
Tattooed drug users facing up to accusers
And abandoned bottles belonging
To a chorus of snoring (mixed with plenty of imploring) –
Coming from a choir of intransigent boozers –
Who can never see that they'll always be the losers –
And a pair of fornicators having to de-camp
Because of his cramp – not helped by localised damp

I spoke to them – in a way not wishing to offend –
As I told them that their squat had been condemned
And that they'd all have to leave –
But a grey haired man the others called Steve,
Said "You'll have to carry me out –
As I'm completely immobile from this blasted gout" –
And his companion added, "Then there's his pneumonia –
Which was echoed by an illegal immigrant from Estonia?"

The place was squalid – strewn with years of old litter –
Of plastic needles and empty cans once full of bitter –
A red haired Irish girl was heard to moan –
"I'll be off to ballet school – if I can only lose five and a half stone –
If not I shall try and sell my story of heart rending distress
To the Sunday papers or the daily tabloid press –
Living well through them – till I become much lighter
With a gin soaked – black country ghost writer."

He had told her his work was investigative
By nature – with a few lines – not lies – 'more of a creative
Bent' – which annoyed me – I was trying to keep calm
All those people most exposed to serious harm
As their unreasonable woes caused by people considered as foes
Must be defused before they all turn to blows –
After all the local police rely on me
To keep this area – underclass free – as they often say –
"Don't quote me – but – here's a few quid to keep crime at bay."

Food Chain

Fleet gazelle
Until felled
By lioness
To swell her cubs –
Jackals as well

The Marble Kid

The marble Kid rolled in
With a graze upon his chin –
I said we'll glaze that graze
Then you'll be good as new –
Just carry on practising
And you'll regain your hue
Of biscuit blue

For rejuvenating your sheen
We'll mix in copper green –
Much it will cost –
But you'll see
A great improvement
'cos this verdigris'
Is claimed 'best there is'

Now renewed –
And filled with gratitude
You can roll about
Like a lout –
With youthful attitude
And head of granite
Conqueror of the marble planet

Oh No I'm Not

Oh no! – Not another Adele's strop
She's always so depressing –
That's why I'm always stressing
That I think she should stop –
And see her life as a blessing
And not continually saying 'I'm not'

I suggested she go for counselling –
She replied never – certainly not –
Last time I got stressed as the Counsellor
Was late for the appointment –
And I like to start on the dot –
Not ringing in with excuses – claiming a lot
Of ill fortune and disappointment
Needing sympathy and cortisone ointment

Besides with the way things are –
For my old car – I wouldn't get very far –
Cos of all those old drivers who should not
Be allowed on the road –
Until they can pass the Highway Code –
Some of them can't see and what's more
They still signal by pre-war semaphore

If I had my way I'd ban old ladies and ban lads –
With the exception – of course – of my granddad –
After all he's a gent – and he lends me his car –
So he'd definitely not be subject to any bar
I'd impose – on those near comatose
Old fools – who confuse their lunch

With the first aid box and end up munching
Their sandwiches with pickles and bandages

I'd not let into the country any
Illegals for a few soon becomes many –
I'd not allow all that banshee howling –
From antisocial foreign clerics prowling
Around – within inner city bounds
And without thinking – I'd ban people
From pubs – I found were not drinking –
And send them on their way – slinking
With all those banshees howling –
And anyone I found scowling

It's not that I'm miserable – I'm not –
It's just that those silly expressions –
Give me manic depressions –
Like getting hitched and tying the knot –
Which I view as a lot of Tommy Rot

White Hedge And Ditch

The vociferous cow parsley – loudly
Calls – as it stains the roadside green and white
Clad thus – in its honest garb worn proudly –
Though not in arrogance – cautiously bright –
As it gives purpose to the hawthorn gown
Towering into an afternoon sky
Sistered with the blackthorn – lace blossom grown
Framed with cow parsley low – dog rose up high

Let us welcome travellers to promenade –
At their leisure – this wayside of delight
Its shear abundance unhid from men – hard
Of purpose in their quest for harvest right
To pick fruits for hedgerow stimulation –
Put to brew for lively fermentation.

Fog's Chill Will

The morning wore a quilt of thick white cloud –
A spread of vapourized – (chilled dust) –
Right to the ground –
Shapelessly fashioned – deadening all sound –
As though charging all to speak below whispers –
While the foggy outcrop – of whitened blisters –
Sat astride thorn rich hedges
To muffle all in rime frost
And dead sunlight – to agriculture's cost

How this vacuous fog marches without sound
Covering ground as though
On manoeuvres –
Spreading chill munificence from fence to fence –
Ordered – cold – unremitting – bleak –
Bound to other words I hear as 'morning speak'
Its asthma – reducing to a squeak –
Fine words of wish and will –
Caught up in gasps of hoary chill

Paraded as a Winter land bound in frozen spite –
Ice takes those short of breath
With cruel asthmatic bite –
Causing them a rasping – gasping discomfort –
They – the un-insured – being most affected –
So poorly – (were they) – protected –
With such little physic selected
To mix or rub or gargle on –
Or protect from risk till germs are done

Let these unprotected souls take the swallows flight
Caused to go – (we believe) to Summer warmth –
So we were told all we need to know –
Hoping frozen spite had relented – sent those afflicted
From asthmatic bite – south to Capricorn –
Not late – or ill fed – nor dead –
It's just that they have gone on ahead –
Away from rime frost
And wet sunlight – to be saved – to be fed
With each of those poor souls once permanently lost

It's In The Papers

It must be true 'cos it's what the Murdoch papers say
Written by reporters steeped in an honourable tradition
So these facts are right – all as printed in the 'Sun' today

Such as all those politicians who fiddled their pay –
With expenses claimed as if given as a pay addition –
It must be true 'cos it's what the Murdoch papers say

Gordon Brown wrote a note in a disrespectful way
To the family of a lad killed by transport omission
So these facts are right – all as printed in the 'Sun' today

He died needlessly in Helmund – there where he lay
From a lack of helicopters and small arms ammunition
It must be true 'cos it's what the Murdoch papers say

Mr Brown's writing is so bad it's put on public display
To show it's been mis-spelt by an eye sight condition
So these facts are right – all as printed in the 'Sun' today

Our lame duck prime Minister has feet of clay
It's serialised and printed in every week day edition
It must be true 'cos it's what the Murdoch papers say
So these facts are right – all as printed in the 'Sun' today

From Weavers To Believers

The oozier lay cut – ready for the weaving
Left at rest – for the weavers were all leaving
Gone with the plough boy –
Lad from the cattle byre
And town brass band playing songs of joy –
On their way to take up a soldier's stance
There – in a foreign extermination mire –
Somewhere out in France

Kitchener's call to arms had stirred
These under achievers and infused them
With spurious rhetoric – turned into believers
In patriotic duty – theirs but to do or die –
Not to cry –
So – not to waste a jot by wondering why

For so many precious young lives
Have been tossed into a cauldron
Without mothers – now with each other –
To be tabulated – unknown –
Where no-one survives –
All youthful hope gone – with breath
Squeezed out – mud-packed –
Neither laid nor stacked –
They – north facing – boots and coats
Gone west – all jest bleached out

All now mulch to feed a madness –
As spit and polish leaches south –
Crammed into death by sloth
Taken in – by word of mouth –

Propaganda has it clear –
How proud their families would be
To retrieve a ragged bag of bones –
In truth – met with cries and groans
At this meagre return to homes –
Buried here – buried there –
In nameless graves – they lie unknown –
With no more breath to spare

Bespoke Armchair

I could sometimes sense
The ghosts of people sitting there –
In my elm and beech arm chair –
Shaped – lathe backed – intact –
Some time "bespoke" –
Designed to attract potential sitters –

Visiting priests, doctors or vicars –
Relations young and old
Sat there – come in from the cold
To sit by the log fire
Burning bright – giving light –
Smelling fresher than coal or anthracite

Dogs and cats curled up
There – on the elm seat – solid –
Never in need of polish or repair –
Once orphaned ducklings – wrapped
In old woollen cloth –
Not long from being "come upon" –
Trapped in baling wire –
Were coddled on that chair –
In their used wool wear –
Warming at the ash log fire

Old (clay pipe) folk sat and dreamed
While kettles chattered and steamed
Hung from steel gibbets –
Or stood on brass pressed trivets –
Making the most of blackened range's
Sparkings and splutterings –
In tune with brier pipe mutterings

Stew pots over wood cinders
Would have often simmered
While frisky kittens skimmered
Beneath the baulk of elm
Sitting on close turned legs –
Within pipe cleansing reach
Of that heavily leaded – kitchen grate

Old cloaks and coats draped
Across her back to dry out
belonging – (no doubt) to those more
fitting to "their chair" than me to "mine" –
Custodian for just a short time –
Only until the chair is re-let
Tenure set to yet "another tenant"
Only for a share of "my"
Beech and elm – "bespoke" armchair

Countryside Care

Shall we care about the countryside?
Her views – her good fresh air –
Where morning comes in with pride –
Dancing – while clad in sunshine ware
Contrasting with darker blots of shade –
So let us care about the countryside
Before her lasting remnants fade

Of the shrinking green belt – good
For poachers – long dog lurchers –
All keepers of the pheasant wood
And timely ornithological searchers
Coming from a noisy urban sprawl
To try to find a hallowed rustic calm
Before the countryside – becomes 'no more'

To seed (the exposed) peat on wild moor
With tufted grasses – that will thrive
As cover for the fiery grouse – core
Game bird – to keep the moor alive
As are – Whimbrel and – Widgeon
Paddling and wading –spading with
Long curved bills with which to 'dig on'

Let soft meadows grow as they will
So insects and birds – in frantic flight –
Can go hunting for their needy fill
Among those loggers and doggers – trite
Cessation of long held hostilities –
So that the countryside does not withdraw
From nature's use and man's abilities

So let us all take care of the countryside
Over snow or under rainbow – with views
Of her various flora sown with pride –
Cowslip yellows and corn flower blues
It's we 'rural guardians' right to choose –
Do the fox and rabbit stay – or go the way
Of Speckled Beauties and Apple Bumblebees

Playin' The Spoons

I met ol' Geoffrey Grinnall
Out one night in June
Playin' a lively air
On a pair of pressed steel spoons –
Where upon I asked 'im
The name of 'is quite merry tune –
To which 'e replied,
"You'll get no golden tan
From a waxin' silver moon."

I asked if 'e was serious –
Or just a takin' the micky out of me –
'e said, "Now that could never be –
For you be a distant cousin –
To whom I must pay worthy due."
I replied, "I'm not so far away –
In fact I'm standin' next to you."

'e seemed somewhat disturbed
At me a sayin' merry tune –
Well 'e 'ad come out to practice
For a funeral that was due quite soon –
So 'e must practice this ol' dirge
With a man that 'e called mate –
Who – I must stress was unknown to me –
But then Ol' Geoff urged me to believe
That 'is mate – was only runnin' late.

"What instrument does 'e play."
I asked politely – bein' a bit concerned
At what ol' Geoff might say –
"Well 'e made it while ''e was interned
In a German prison camp."
So that's why ''e calls it 'is balloom –
I asked, "Why on earth does ''e call it that?"
Geoff said, "'cause he made it from
A flush valve ball an' the 'andle off a broom."

I stood there for a while – not wishin' to intrude
Just a listenin' quietly – till 'e dropped a spoon –
Then I realized it 'ad words that were very rude –
But on mentioning this – 'e called out at me – 'you buffoon' –
'e then showed me a note from the undertaker
Where was written beneath the date
The details of the poor deceased – which I read out
To ol' Geoff – Who gasped, "Well by name it be me mate."

I muttered my ill prepared condolences
An' offered to try an' play 'is mate's balloom –
But Geoff thought this a poor idea
Akin to a marriage without a groom –
Which was 'ow 'is mate's weddin' was –
When 'is wife 'ad to get married on 'er own
For 'is mate was in the casualty after
Trippin' – on the front door mat
A causin' 'im a breakin' several bones
"Well this be 'is funeral," Ol' Geoff then said,
"An' – with a bit of luck – 'e won't be late for that."

The Caracal

The caracal gave vent
To his hunger dissent –
Over a carcass meant
For his family – spent
On hunting game –
That the jackal
Had taken in shame
And will never relent.
So the raging went –
In apportioning blame –
Against claim and
Counter claim – bent
On fear's scent –
To judge thieving intent
Before the advent
Of coming lent
And common hunger
For the younger
Issue

Serviceable

The bridge that spans
Serves more
That broken one
In two parts –
It hangs

The Tea Towel Kidnap Mystery

Following a party at my home, one of my guests took a number of tea towels in order to launder them. After many months and the involvement of Interpol my towels were returned anonymously, beautifully laundered.

I lost a group of true old friends
From a party called for making amends –
Though they may be thread bare
I was used to having them take care
Of certain household chores
Washing up – though never used on floors.

How they chattered to be back
Learning that they had not had the sack –
Blue and white check tearily cried
Relieved to have PG Tips back by his side
So it was that National Trust
Agreed to share a drawer with them – if he must

They told me that they had been taken
By an Australian for wrapping boiled bacon –
She called it taking them into care
She had insisted that they wash their hair
Then spun dried them rapidly –
Bagged them up in a carrier – haphazardly

I asked them if they would charge
Her for removing them from the world at large
Surprisingly they all said no
Because she'd taken them with so
Much good intent that if I did not demur
They would ask to be allowed to be sent back to her

Wood Nymph's Day

My washing danced upon the line
In a morning turned out fine
Until a sudden fall of hail
Filled up the pockets on my coat
Which then fell on my goat –
In a wind that blew like a gale.

The rabbit ate the chocolate cake
That I was asked if I would bake
For the birthday of twin elves.
Now I have to go without a gift
Because without a lift –
I can't reach the other from the shelves.

The rocking horse no less
Had made a smelly mess
From underneath it's tail.
I swept the large intruders up –
Far bigger than a coffee cup –
No wonder he looked pale.
My faithful yellow slip on shoe

Mated with a stray of royal blue
So my new pumps came in two shades of green –
One a bright florescent lime
The other as dark as autumn thyme
Most super shoes I've ever seen.

So I put on my bright yellow hose
Stretching from my whatsits down to my toes
And then, shod in different greens
I set of in a cream tam o' shanta
That I received last year from Santa
And went as a comport of beans.

I was judged in with the vegs
By a druid called Hedges
Who said, "What a pleasant surprise –
I'll give you a highly commended
For the way you've contended"
Then awarded me a rotten third prize.

I collected my winnings
Which paid for the beginnings
Of my anti addiction lessons –
But the way that I smoke
I told that psychiatrist bloke
I'm sure I'll need many more sessions.

The Grey Judge

The grey judge of winter
Pores over my indictments –
Calling on law books
And a great many more books –
Finally he decides to jettison
His greyness – his frayedness
As part of my redress –
In a freezing by breezing
Collarless hair suit of ice –
Put on to clear me of vice

Discontented as unrepented
I fight for appeal and window seal
With the crafts that put paid to drafts
For moribund is my repair fund
Clashing with regret over debt
That holds up the action
With an improper fraction

How arithmetically entered
I have – as yet – not heard from dissenters
I feel are most likely –
To have invoked the Almighty –
Gaining his backing
Before they are all put on his list
For their sacking –
Agreeing to a wages subtraction
Carried out by an improper fraction

Harvest Light

A pattern appeared across the way
In the field where they were making hay
Fresh geometric lines – laid from the blade –
Dappled by afternoon sun and shade –
Making a tartan of verdant hues – past noon –
Just where May danced into June

Such a time brings heartfelt jollity
Bordering (at times) on frivolity –
Where the rambler's march is held –
At the gate where a tree was felled
Last Michaelmas – taking its place
Anew – as laid low in fallen grace
Was a worthy sapling – grappling
With becoming a 'new tree' happening

So the autumn gathering begins –
New harvest now stored in bulky metal bins –
Where once the farmyard barn was king
Storing bales of straw bound up with string –
Flailed grain – onions – beets and roots
Piled high where September's lively shoots
Lie – compressing August's salve
Now only memories on the empty shelves

But there are still patterns painted on our minds
Holding work (from our youth) – of all kinds
Of circles – flailed by the reapers wooden sails
Cut into the dusty haze – hanging over bales
Of barley straw – of wheat and fresh mown hay –
Compressed so tightly – filling every bay
And if we listen hard we can hear the hooves
Of horses echoing – beneath old stone slate roofs

So patchwork and circles claw their way –
Through our minds to such days of making hay –
Methods and folk more earnest then – in sweat –
Forcing aching limbs to targets that must be met –
So to feed their families and themselves
With a harvest home that filled those shelves –
Where once again we'd caper to a comely tune
With wenches – just where May danced into June

A Night With Purcell

There was a paleness that ran
Across his graceful west face –
As if the heavens had cause to scan
St James – caught in a moonlit chase –
His silvered edifice
Was vessel to a golden sound –
Where a local gathering sat enthused
With the joy of music –
Both infusive and profound
I went to only one performance

I had been to several – years before –
There I sat and wished I had attended more –
If only for the romances
Created by musicians with bows on strings
Joined by a soprano who sang
With voice on wings – that sold me
On their flight to Henry Purcell –
She and they lifted my spirits perfectly well

Exorcised my melancholy –
Interspersed with musical jollity –
Baroque notes on viol a family
Of strings – brings a musical homily
Ending not in bluster but gusto –
There to remind me that I must go –
As I did several years before –
And attend many more
Concerts – such searching musical sound
Made my enjoyment –
Amongst such studious company
All the more profound

Grizzled

Old Man Lingers
Poor of gait
Legs Far from strait
Uses stick – held
In arthritic fingers

The Wisdom Of Gran

I often used to go round to my Granny Hughes
She was wise and enjoyed a fair exchange of views –
"When was Edward George's time Gran?
I have to write an essay
on the times of this uncommon man –
For 'not paying attention when I am in class'
And being disruptive
with a very comely lass"

"Well when our new English teacher,
whom I call Miss Crimes,
First came in, she introduced herself as Miss Rimes
And so I said 'with this' and a mildly rude word
Not one of the 'holy trinity' of expletives Gran,
it's so absurd.
Oh! and being caught looking at Claire Clegg's long legs –
And merely remarking she had a pair of very shapely pegs."

Ignoring my remarks Gran concentrated and then perspirated
As she related a tale about a man who'd been implicated
In some scandal or other – or maybe – p'raps it wasn't him –
It could have been his younger brother – Tim – or was it Jim –
Whoever it was couldn't explain,
when forced into taking the blame,
Just how he had come by the contents of the squire's cold frame,
And some very good examples of freshly shot course game

She went on "Well now it could have been that rag and bone man
Who had a peculiar wife – I think he called her Jan.
They came from Blockley –
I'm sure his name was Edward George.
Always parked his cart round at the back of the Westington forge.
His wife used to say he was a fine goods courier –
'Til he started buyin' rabbit skins –
Then she referred to him as a quite exclusive furrier.

During the war there was an Edward George
responsible for changed the clocks –
Or was he the cabinet member
responsible for shortened women's frocks?
No! I think he could have been
the minister to do with cotton socks
Wait now – ah yes –
he was something to do with the countries docks."

"Stevedore Gran," I offered as my attempt at helping out.
In an exasperated response she growled
"What are you going on about.
I don't know whether his name was Steve or Dora
or something else altogether."
I enquired "Perhaps he was responsible for all of that bad weather"
"Bad weather in deed,
what you need my lad is a taste of some good leather.
Where else did you misbehave at school today?" She impugned.
"Well in 'RI' I was blamed when Jimmy Dither mooned"

"And Miss Serene – 'that old has been'
didn't like my choral reference,
Saying that it didn't show the Lord due deference
Because when the class sang
'Onward Christian soldiers going as to war'
I sang 'Oh! my blistered shoulders they are very sore.'
Their second line was 'With the cross of Jesus going on before'
While I sang 'I must take this sun block and rub it on some more.'
It's not my fault Gran – I've never been able to learn by rote.
And that's what gets those teachers' goat

Gran seemed bemused but said, "Are you sure you're not confused?
This Edward George man could be men.
We had Kings – an Edward and a George
and then Edward and George again"
I didn't like the way things were leading,
So I decided to brighten up proceedings

"Listen Gran I know a funny joke –
It's much better than any you get from all them WI women folk."

> The other day Jimmy's Dad shot their cockerel
> While it was a cock-a-doodling
> Jimmy asked why did you do that Dad?
> His father replied
> To stop him crowing – far too much 'fowl' language Lad

Gran stood up and said, "I've got a headache lad.
It's a real thumper – this one's really bad –
I shall take some medicinal whisky and retire to my bed."
Much concerned I enquired,
"What's the matter Gran – was it something that I said?

My Granddad

My Granddad taught me gardening –
And other things besides –
Like what to do with they young girls
While out on hay cart rides –
Give them a frolic in the bales but never
Leave them cause to think
That any of them will be your bride

For you my rustic lad are setting out
On an un-fair journey –
Where wives now have the upper hand
An' Lad I must warn 'e
To keep your guard in place – for
You might be called
To face – a wily women's lib attorney

Though I felt Granddad must be right –
Well 'e said 'e always was –
It didn't help me with my courtin' plight
As I'd lost my chattin' buzz
So now I had to seek advice from elsewhere
Like in the 'Sheaf n' Shupick'
Which was what we gardener's alus does
'Cos you gets some good advice when down the pub

When considerin' plantin' our best seeds –
We double-digs so gently
Cos we plants many more seed than is needed
Above a score – that's twenty –
So it is with girls – one's alus one too much
But a lad must test 'em all
Not yet knowin' one is more than plenty –
In fact any of 'em is far too many

A Holiday In Malta

I have a good friend named Mandy –
Who arranged a divorce very handy –
So I could not easily fault her
When learning – she's planned a holiday
With her ex – over the sea in Malta.

At first I was slightly aghast
So much so – that she laughed –
Saying, "We'll sleep on our own –
Though in a twin bedded room
And his mother will be chaperone.

She could see I wasn't convinced
As she winced –
"His mother insisted she must sleep on her own
And – as we have only two rooms
We're forced into sleeping together – alone."

"Two weeks of displaying each other's bits
Will have you both at the end of your wits."
I said with a grin –
"And it's no good relying on fate
Or his Mother – butting in."

"It only needs just enough booze
To light the old dampened fuse –
And you could be off on bedroom gymnastics
Stripping down to your dripping –
While tripping a new light fantastic.

Though I suppose Malta is handy
For the sharing of a portion of mid-night candy
And although this action is Cheltenham's loss
It will surely remind Malta
Why they earned – their much prized George Cross.

Demise Of Rhyme And Metre

There were more patches of witches grass
That shone like polished candle brass
In the middle of my saddening mind –
Called such as it could no longer find
A cause for rhyme or call for metre

So no more rhyme – no more metre –
No shape – nor form there to meet her –
As she requests verse in form that will
Meet well – with penny educated masses
And afterwards polish candle brasses

Travel well with single furrowed plough
Or in the sty farrowing an awkward sow –
Perhaps in giving and taking from the loam
No! – nor sung at the final harvest home

Stilted in construction and introduction
But printed – rightly priced – in production
So used well on witches patchy grass
And to shine old polished candle brass

All done without the use of rhyme or Metre
Though I hear the spirits failed to greet her –
Once it was know the black demons beat her
Without her old friends – Rhyme and metre

Note:
I still feel Little Miss Free-verse would be so much sweeter – if pampered by my two friends – Rita Rhyme and Maureen Metre

Disturbing

Stumbling – bumbling
Mind racing
Heart chasing –
Feet pacing
Stomach rumbling –
Throat grumbling –
Grunts unceasing –
Most Displeasing
In their rampaging
For morsels – raging –
In chronic moans
Against those hormones
That let it be chewed –
Downed – as food.
Abhorring ravings –
Turning to cravings
For morsels –
In forestalling
That which is much more.

Pane Of Glass

Though I'm sealed in
It is not the reason I can't be seen
For I am protection in between
The hostile air
And managed – conditioned fair
I am a friend to light
As it comes and goes
Through the day and night.

Some times I feel my work's demeaning
But only when I'm in need off cleaning.
Fuss me – buff me – let me gleam
And keep me away from steam
For I wish to spend my days
Un-cracked or crazed
In order never to be seen.

Fleetingly Non-Memorable

They – the good and great
Look down on us – from
Their steel and glass towers –
Air conditioned –un-inhibited –
Multiplying their time and take
By 'tip glass' hours –
Calculated by using –
Free running sand showers.
How – I wonder – will I stride –

Under the weight of all their pride
And make a successful bid
To enter in to those alien
Steel and glass – anti-palientalian –
Ergonomically friendly –
Morphic resonanced – unendingly
Passing from PhD to PhD
By-passing the likes of you and me

Let my dallyings be
The food of procrastination
To further my chance of assimilation
Into these towers of Babel
Applying by e-mail or maybe by cable –
Blackberry – or blue tooth –
Or any other such uncouth –
Technological ingrate –
So quickly outdated
And (thought by me) much overrated
Systems – ephemeral
And – hopefully – fleetingly –
Becoming non-memorable

No Scene

Blow aerial down
Teams play –
Score goals unseen
On corrupted screen –
Ruins cup final day
Mid-May

Darker End Of day

At the darker end of day
Poor sight laid a lance of pale moonlight
Against a bale of hay –
Sliding shiftily through a half open door –
To lie upon the dry mud floor

So nocturnal stirrings rouse
The snouted night-shift legions – to attack
Evening's constant grouse –
On their search for victuals that they lack –
Behind day's darkened back

So the priestly mole –
Clad in (cassock black) tunnelling clothes –
Trundled in subterranean hole –
Urging forceful ripping claws to expose
His skyward pointing nose

As nocturnal creatures
Tread softly on a crush of leaf mould dross –
Those frosty crispened features –
Now (down fallen) cover – over lichen moss –
And are first of autumn's loss

So night slips in with ease –
Lit by poor moonlights pale primrose shard –
Caught by defoliated trees
Above the monochrome legions – charred
By nightfall's tarry yard

So life grinds round
In moonlit chases – after sustenance or prey –
For sup – is to be found
Where a moonlight spear lies on a bale of hay –
At dusk – the darker end of day

What's Wrong With Me?

I demanded to know what was wrong with me
To which he replied, "Well! besides your stroke
Which was nothing to fret about – you see –
Because it happens to so many other folk –
Please be reassured – I'm sure you'll agree –
That your chronic back pain just needs a soak –
And we've just diagnosed emphysema
Which rhymes (almost) nicely with leukaemia"

Bulbous neck and upper body glands
Swelled by dysfunctional lymphocytes
Are running down like beaded bands
To take the shape of mistimed mosquito bites
Showing on shoulder blades and hands
Others ringing aorta's splice – well out of sight
While overlapping osteophytes result is ankylosis
So we need to check for signs of a thrombosis

Don't worry – we can hold your body stable
With regular doses of paracetamol which matches
Well with senna to help your bowels be able –
Acting in tandem with co-proxiamol batches
And amlodopine which won't disable –
The good effect of buprenorphine patches
While candesartan and amitripyline
Will help to keep you systems clean

I tried to leave but needed a helping hand
From the nurse – who observed – somewhat wryly,
"I'm surprised you have the strength to stand
And the way you bear yourself I view most highly" –
As she rolled my appointments in an elastic band
And handing them to me – smiling somewhat shyly
I smiled back –winching as she said, "We need more blood
For the last three lots turned out to be no good."

My Lady Of The Light

A fine looking woman came before my eyes
Such an effect she had on me –
I was there – in a state – somewhere
Between mesmerised and paralysed –
If I was breathalysed in this guise
I would be charged as being empty –
For if they knocked upon my chin –
They'd find that there was no-one in

She was delightful – dressed in calico and lace
With no make-up on her face –
Wore only a serene look of certain calm –
A humble expression of fair grace –
Being that of an angelic harpsichordist
Sent from – I know not where – as a sharp recordist
Playing quietly as she touches hammers onto strings –
Inducing a relaxing of old guards – and all things that it brings

Pleasure and my felicitous girl go together
So well her personage is – as sunny weather –
Bringing capriciousness to staid audiences
As she adulterates their gravitas and importances –
Lets the burdens of life move over to the walls
While minds and imaginations take command
of the centres of compliant halls
And so making merry begins with earnest play –
Allowing a little (sporting) cavorting to take the day

So (as day follows day) she flies me to St John's
On to Copacabana then to racing at Le Mans –
Quickly on to Florence – David and their surrounds
A carpet ride to Tripoli and here battle grounds –
Gallipoli – followed by a Greek Island tour
Of Lesbos – Delos – Patmos and many more –
Before landing back (so gently) from our cruise –
So she kissed and left me – to my world educing snooze

I see the sun shines brighter whenever she appears
The flowers (in the borders) grow much faster
than they did in other years
In response to her urging ways and the longer days –
For she is an April arrivée called upon to use her inveterate rays
So night is replaced – by my Lady of Sun Light

Seasonal Games

We children played our seasonal games
Hopscotch – marbles and others without names
Chasing in fields – chastising a plethora of thorns –
Avoiding large beasts with very large horns –
Countenancing hawkers who strode as tall men
Listening to talkers who trod as very small men –
Rounding bonfires built up of some garden waste
In which we roasted potatoes – hard to the taste

Night-time in November seemed glorious –
Cascades of pleasure bordering on uproarious –
In rain fog and cold – it's as alike as sunshine –
All our days were those days of roses and wine
Served up to us in adolescence – before pain
Cut us to the size of those who moaned when it rained –
Without hopscotch or marbles or brown paper kites
And without any desire to rush into fights

Men are not just big boys playing with big boys toys
They are people who can't stand a great deal of noise
Vulnerable – greying – balding –and many arthritic –
Who – no longer are able to play football or cricket –
So now they are drawn to watching sky sports
Viewing from the bar or with smoking shed sorts
All now free to criticize the blokes who still play
Saying as how these blokes would never have survived
If they'd had to play on the pitches we had in our day

So I wonder – just how much worse it can get?
Before all those 'to highly paid' sportsmen are let
Go before they start – in case they become liabilities
Before they have the chance to ruin those new facilities
Put in on the insistence of the health and safety chap
Who is judged in his absence as being a large pile of crap
I would certainly dislike all of those old men
If it weren't for the fact that I'm one of them

Barge Balked

The mare stumbled
Barge stalled
Lock gate lifted –
Water poured
Un-sifted – over
Those un-moored
Lives – uninsured

Stand Again

I wish that they could stand again –
Those brave mistreated Campden men
And – that I could stand with them –
Those long defeated Campden men –
To give as them – at their own expense –
All dried up in need of drench
That fearful thirst calling for a quench
And a way out from that awful trench
Sadly there can never be such a strategy
For them or me – as we exist independently –
They have been and seen and gone
While I – at this sunrise am let live on –
Soon to travel where those brave men wend
Left to settle at another centuries end

Woodruff And Wintergreen

Woodruff and Wintergreen bloom well
But beware of Creeping Jenny –
As does the Scarlet Pimpernel –
First of many

Adder's tongue and Hoary Alison
Make love-in-a-mist – floral tryst –
Spreading cloth to put challis on –
One of many

Touch-me-not – cried blue-eyed-Mary
In Lady's-mantle of fescue –
As April's reds and yellows vary –
Some of many

So it remains that Stitchwort thrives –
Hartstongue and saxifrage speedwell –
While Sweet Cicely and couch come to life –
Best of many

City Lights

Dazzling eyes
Un-accustomed
To the sharpness
Of the neon hell
Wish they were
Back as soon
As can be arranged
By bus or train
Under solitary
Lambing moon

Witness Flowers

The skies – which discharged their wrath
Saw inclement weather – come by rain –
Though the rain stayed not – running off
To spiral down the thirsty purple drain.
The squall intensified to soak and maul
And drench outside – the gathering pack
Scurrying – as if falling from a cliff –
By now in mid flight – with no way back –
Having been subjected to a winter's toll
So bleak it makes weak a springtime goal

(All aborting) creatures of their own fright
Are glad – when sunshine breaks the day
By burning off the grey and greyer light –
Baking the wake of inclemency's foul play
And heralding the buds of drops and bells –
To parade in hedgerows – fields and woods
Away from conifers thick – 'light thieving'
Overcoats – that let go the snow in floods –
As blue and white survivors of winter's toll
Lead us out – to our springtime goal

Despite all – the meadows gird their loins
And profuse their May-time stages with
Balletic ferns – buttercups and daisies –
While the woodlands wild garlic goes on show
As a mature succulent worthy of the speaking –
So thick – it – like snow in springtime fazes –
Though almost ousted by the blue bell seeking
Shade – carpeted in (knee high) woodland baize
As the drenched and wayward gathering pack
By now in flight – to find their own way back
From winter's dark and freezing toll
To reach (an often dreamt of) – springtime goal

Senders Of Cards

A string of envelopes fell flat
On the front hall mat
Signalling the on-set
Of Christmas cheer –
All over again this year

Maybe they could call
In for a chat – though
My house is small –
Over time – I could
Accommodate them all

So all you senders of cards
Call in for your rewards –
Mince pies – mulled wine
And a short call on your time
Which all of you can easily afford

Cast out cards – save rain forests –
Speak your words of best
Wishes – when face to face
Under mistletoe swishes –
While tasting seasonal kisses

Breath in the clear – winter air –
Think of things to say –
Bring things we each can share –
Practice talking on your way
As though it's a coat you love to wear

Let chatter get the better
Of each written letter –
While you're here with me
And take – with seasonal glee –
A gift – from my well wishers tree

Pauline

Dear Pauline
You were born
To combat scorn –
Show a sense of fun
In the way you always
Get things done

To wash the devil away –
Brighten up the coming day
So – if I may – I'd like to say
Thanks to you Pauline –
You are in every way

A loaner out of swimming pools
Not a gladly sufferer of fools –
But concerned for those
Who drool – a carer
But never wearer
Of heart on sleeve –
Always on the way
Never having
just been
You are to
One and all
A consummate Caring Queen

Note:
Author's thanks to Pauline Twiselton, former Chair of Campden Voluntary Help Group

Delightfully

Delightfully she looked at me –
Or was she looking at the tree
That shaded me –which ever –
She did it so disarmingly

I was certain to be impressed
For as she looked – she smiled
Softly – it was the softness
Of the smile that beguiled me

So pleasantly she shaped her face
I invested my love in her grace –
I asked her for a dance – politely –
She held my advance delightfully

She spoke softly – pleasantly to me
Or perhaps to the tree that sheltered me
I wondered wistfully if it could be me
Or that shady parasol – of a hiring tree
That brought her to smile – so disarmingly

How And Where

Where do I live!
Do I live or am I dead?
If alive then sorely weaned
On sour milk and drier bread.

How do I breath!
Do I breathe, or do I choke?
If breathing then I suffocate
On fog and belching smoke.

Where now are they!
Where are they, who left me here?
If here, then well hid
But still they hold my fear.

How does God choose!
Does God choose wisely?
If wise then without an explanation
His wisdom does deride me.

Where has reason gone?
Has reason gone to hide?
If gone to hide then who - in hell
Does reason sit beside.

Old Bill

There is old Bill sat
In his house content by day
Of rest which is assured –
Till lone brass blows him away.
Better now – they say
As they pray –
Than he was yesterday –
Now he's been called away

Play Up And Play the Game

It was an indifference of knowledge –
For she had gone off to collage –
Such dash clipping my natural ardour –
Lessening my usual candour
To a more covert presentation
Of my opinion – on her education

For she knew much more than me –
Upon this fact we mostly disagree
But she benefits from higher education
And I from only fits of secondary degradation

I now proclaim it's such a shame
That she's so small while I – rather tall –
Are disproportionately 'ismed' when playing ball
On that seconded green and levelled playing field
That she craves for – causing me to yield
Away from my principled playing up
To play up – play up and play the game

For she has more support that me –
Upon this claim we mostly disagree
But she benefits from legislation
As I suffer more regulation irritation

I would like to stand my ground
And claim equality in the round –
But I'm disbarred as no minority ethnic
Would be – by my protestant work hard ethic –
I claim that when I go it will be a happy release
Until I'm told I no longer have the right to die in peace

Slow March (Bearers)

In memory of Robert Hawkins, a Pebworth Fireman

Wooden box filled with sand bags
Wrapped in rags –
The six – perplexed faced – bearers
Took – with care –
A handle each and on the hushed
Command – pushed
The dead weight into the air –
Each pair
Learning the sad art of slow march –
Not to lurch
First inside leg forward – slowly put –
Outside foot
Following with soft rhythmic boot –
Done to suit
The task of sadness now rehearsed –
The first
Of more nights round and round
Till found
That respectful sense of oneness –
As in dress
Respectful for him – the other one
Their tread – a trudge neatly done
Complete until the day
All can rest now until Friday comes
When seven chums
All together – as one – one more time –
Six in their prime –
Honouring a respected colleague
One more time – for all time

Sun Light On Stone

How the evening sun
Anoints the mellow masonry
With a soft – rich pink
Which – by curfew bell –
The limestone carries well

Held in a sunset that is
Always true –
To shade and hue –
Lemons and carnations –
Corals and other permutations
Of khakis and greys –
Depending on the weather
And the time of day

Let these moments linger –
When the sun light
And stone walls
Mingle – in such a sheer delight –
Such an emotive sight

Circus Head

A circus lives inside my head
With imps and chimps all dressed in red
Misers – Tigers – Lions too
Dressed in gold and navy blue –
Elephants decked in shocking pink
With only time enough to blink

As we the penny wise
Sat (for all the world) quite mesmerised
By noisy clowns and acrobats, their up's and down's
Performed in bronze and silver gowns
While Jugglers played with golden crowns

There are dancing bears with purple hair –
Morose tumblers who just sit and stare
With three blind mice – one smaller –
one taller and a third called Paula

A Yorkshire terrier bitch
Tight-rope walked without a glitch
Then lost her precious pitch to a rare technical hitch –
Causing a sunshine plumber to spread
Marmalade upon his balding head

A Welsh ringmaster young and keen –
And his great aunt Maureen
(dressed in Mauve with a silver sheen)
Both shed tears for a partner whom they'd never seen –
Who once romanced her with seedy antics
Which she mistook for true romantics

Now as I tire I decide to hire a colourful rainbow
To promote another urbane show
With Cossack forces on white horses –
Dressed in navy blue and scarlet corsets
Before they are all packed off to bed –
Where they belong – inside my head

Cancerous Cells

Hidden here – within
A smooth and pale skin
Are microscopic sparks –
Noiseless barks
Sailing – assailing
Capsizing home –
Changing – re-arranging
Textures – mixtures
Grouping – swooping
Over lifelong fixtures –
From time to time
High winds
Drawn out – examined
For their crime –
Unexpungable beacons
In no ordered sequence –
Rogues no longer
At their play
Now seeking prey

Riding Choice Rollers

To ride life's rollers well
Out of hiding – out of hell –
Stay away from water's lane
Tarry not with histrionics
Set out as large waves fain –

To settle for calmer seas – never
Crueller waters – that have
Taken so seriously
All that it could shake free
Like fruit taken from an apple tree
So from my being – while
I'm reeling from my feelings
So forlorn – freshly torn

Sadly rolled into hell –
Though good advice warned
'Steer clear of the devilish sea –
Steer through calmer waters
Far from hidings out of Hades' –
They as with calm – are renewed
In seriousness – but are now
Keeping those Water Street
Travellers far away from harm

So is ranting calmed by charm –
My Muse's charm of serenity
Displacing spilt disparity
With her comparity
So is my well
So my Muse can tell whoever
Tests – we without rest –
Will gain summer best –
Summer dressed

Self Doubt

A priestly parchment – was loudly read –
It's loquacity causing me to scratch my tired head –
My grounding in self doubt
At once twisting – stretching – leeching out –
Partially calling –
From behind a warmth of walling –
I was in torment –
Not knowing exactly what
Theological law meant

For long is the road of learning
And once on it there is little room for turning –
As I have often found to my cost
Quickly becoming lost
Embattled – de-chatteled – rattled –
Caught in disbelief
The theological message becoming far from reach
My disbelief beginning to leech
As though milked by a psychic thief

Fuelled by a belated heraldic vision –
Seeming to bear out the variations
Of my roving beliefs
Often come to grief – starved of relief –
Rationed of courtly passion –
Clawed red by jealousy
Cloaked by the stoically medieval doctrines
Guarded zealously by a priesthood –
professing to do me good –
Routing out all my self doubt
Requiring blind faith –
Succumbing to their unromantic message
Loudly read –
Causing me once more – to scratch my weary head

A Giggle Of Nurses

I went to the doctors t'other day
Where I came upon a giggle of nurses
That put me in mind of May –
Not the month y'understand –
But a very friendly wench
Who was born to a single mother –
Sat on our village bench

These nurses they be very 'elpful
Sorts of girls – an' very cheerful too
They radiates fine pleasantries
As young women often do –
A greetin' folk most cheerily –
Never responding wearily
Even when a' askin' –
Now what can I do for you?

They has no trouble with the needle
When they'm a takin' blood
An if you asks 'em what it's for
They just sez don't you worry lad
Cos this'll do y' good
As one young nurse once said –
An' she said it with a smile –
Hold on for just one more minute
While I fills up another glass blood vial

So all you fellow pensioners
Get round to the doctor's for the flu
Injection – either Asian or the Aysum
It don't matter as they often mix the two
An' they nurses be just as good
At puttin' liquids in to you –
As when they takes out blood –
Cos they girls will tell y'
Both – will help to stop the flu

Ol' Stan reckons 'e be 'alf empty
Since they drained 'im down –
They said they needed to take so much
To make it – a worthwhile trip to town –
So if y' 'ears 'em a gigglin'
You knows your treatment will be good –
But try t' get ''em t' cure you
Without a takin' any blood

Hands Of Spades

A hand of spades without court cards
Only handles and blades stood readily by
As corpses stood devoid of even
Any of life's most innocent ideas –
And died in tears
Each one wondering why –
As the funeral mechanics
All stood quietly by

The condolences read
The prayers finally said –
The spades took up their work
After the mourners had splashed
Handfuls of fine clay over the lashed
Down casket lid – chanting ashes to ashes
Dust to dust – If the Lord doesn't take 'em
Then the devil must

While indolent sexton and assistant
Wielded their hands of spades – blades
In cutting mode slicing spoil
Come out of the six by six feet slot
As poor grade soil
Each one wondering why –
As funeral mechanics
They stood by

They were not seen as
A fitting part of this play –
As their spades took up work
Once the mourners finally spread
Handfuls of fine clay down at the head
Below the casket lid – "Now it was clay clumps."
Said two chumps – "And if our spades don't turn to rust
We'll finish the job". They idley cussed

Dancing In France

So good luck to those boys whom I once saw dance
They're being kept fit in a far away gym
Somewhere near the Somme River – over in France

They joined up while there was still a chance
Of bagging a Hun (honourably) by shooting him
So good luck to those boys whom I once saw dance

By now they'll be wrapped in Passchendaele romance
While military rations are keeping them slim
Somewhere near the Somme River – over in France

We can tell by the papers just with a glance
Charging over the top keeps our lads well in trim
So good luck to those boys whom I once saw dance

I hear many of them have died by bullet or lance
But the graves they're in are all kept tidy and prim
Somewhere near the Somme River – over in France

Our Tommy (just back) said – they no longer prance
Without any arms or legs – times are painfully grim
So good luck to those boys whom I once saw dance
Somewhere near the Somme River – over in France

Flickering Fire Light

A leveret took flight
Across the course rutted –
Ridge and furrow field –
Subjugated by enclosure
And the need – for
A higher tonnage yield

Much to the delighted
Muddy Springer spaniel –
More usually spotted –
In a coat of Black and white –
Determined to bring halt
To that leveret's
(Nervous taken) flight

I called him to my side
But would never chide
Him – for his interest
In this uneven test –
So we turned away
From the falling edge of day –
Returning to the hearth –
There to recall
The young hare's plight –
By the steady red –
Of flickering fire's light

My Wheelbarrow

My wheelbarrow's squeak
Got louder towards the end of every week –
A lack of oil and too much toil where –
Undoubtedly a contribution
To my barrows diminution

My garden hoe has become too slow
And – I think my fork tines
No longer sink as deep as they're supposed to –
With less weight from heel and toe –
So now I leaves my garden fallow

For my wheelbarrow is now weak
With barely an audible squeak –
And my fork and hoe've gone into decline –
All three – worthy friends of mine –
Now in retirement inside the garden shed
As are the gardening plans
That went round inside my 'once keen' head

Oh for those planting lines we made –
The seeds we sowed – the weeds we flayed
The bread and cheese and cider –
Bird scarring 'string and paper glider' –
And at the end of each thoroughly fruitful day –
There was the barrow – filled with dried out weeds
That we merrily wheeled away

Warbled Warning

How deft the dunnock dances
On the apple bough
His busy chirping seems meant
To sound alarm somehow –
Perhaps it is the hawk
Hovering over head –
Or the prowling feral cat
That fills him full of dread.

Thus flustered in his industry
Of collecting grass and straw –
He is filled with such alarm
It shakes him beak and claw –
For he is no match for hawk
In aerial engagement flack –
Just as he measures not –
Up to a wily cat attack.

He warbles out his sole alert –
While about his personal busyings
In hope that he can convey
To all – his strong misgivings –
For left to their own unawares
Without recourse to loud alarm –
They are all in (double) jeopardy
From hawk – or cat's intended harm.

Humour In Health Care

I demanded to know what was wrong with me
Well – he spoke – apart from your stroke
Which is nothing for anyone to fret about –
'cos it happens to so many folk –
Please – be reassured – perhaps not a lot –
I'm a doctor who carries some clout

Will this trust be taken by mouth –
Intravenously or with a spoonful of doubt –
I aggravated him – baited him –
Charged him with being untruthfully grim
"Please don't fret." He replied –
"If you read an obituary in the papers –
You can be sure it's not you who's died."

I was not reassured nor convinced –
For my back hurt so much – I once again winced –
It was not noticed by any medical staff
Though clearly seen – for it brought a laugh –
Half heartedly I must admit –
But definitely a chuckle from a very strange wit

A fit probationary nurse
Wore a broad smiled when she observed –
'I was looking much worse' –
Though not nearly as ill as the man
They'd discharged yesterday –
For he was taken off in the coroner's van

The doctor said I've looked into your file
Not good – of that there's no denial –
But I've noticed you have leukaemia
And a bout of emphysema –
Not to worry though –given the time –
A poet like you could almost
Make those two conditions – rhyme.

Ink And Magenta

How slender are the beams of light
That craze the darkness of the night –
Falling onto colour bled leaves
Of ageing English hardwood trees –
A confusing thread of illumination
Tipping over a brick grey connotation –
Without light – just ink and pitch spilt
Over a marzipan and magenta quilt

Of retreating early sunset – put out
Beyond the western terminator's bout
Of night-time greed – where nocturnal
Mouths devour grubs and seeds and turn all
Unseen leaves drifting down from high reach
Ash, birch and sycamore – oak and beech
Complete the unheard fall to loamy floor
Where darkness marks them with an underscore

To make sure each year they do the same
Playing that (night time) slender lighting game –
Falling on to round stooked barley sheaves
Put up to be dried by westerly August breeze –
In nature's time and place and instigation –
Any other way would cause recrimination
From keepers of granaries specially built
And only half filled – from crops whose seed heads sadly wilt

Marbles, Conkers And Kites

Among my childhood delights
Were marbles – conkers and kites –
Coming into season like dogs and ferrets
Each with it's own set of merits –
No-one knew how we began –
The day the week from when they ran
Seeming to simply just appear –
Universally accepted as being hear

Marbled glass – bulls eyes of every hue
With which you win from me – then I from you –
Played tightly – claimed by the day
All too soon pocketed or simply fading away
On the green – in the gutter
Chinks or potsy I hear you mutter
Better the colours seemed to appear
As better aim means more marbles you clear

Conkers was a series of combative bouts
With very few rules and a flurry of clouts –
Involving three-ers and two-ers
And baked ones and ten-ers and fewers
Pierced by skewers and laced on a string
By knobbly kneed gladiators giving their conkers a fling –
Before 'kick-the-can' took over by night
Lit by a full moon and (gas) street light

The can was kicked – the game was fixed
Teams not selected but randomly mixed –
As we sinewy 'paras' rolled up our 'chutes'
And moved quietly in 'silent-stud' boots
Swiftly over lawns – through cabbages
Tough combatants beating war's ravages
And people at doors starring into the night air
Querying 'that's funny! There's no-one there'
Before returning to a favourite fireside chair

No need to floodlight a brown paper kite
With Radio Times tail and long handling string – for greater height
We took on March winds strong enough
To bowl along tins – bins and litter rough –
Let free with nonsense – to dance
With us 'high wind apostles' and enhance
Our own world with childhood delights
Such as –.marbles – conkers and kites

Four Legged Pest

I saw a thief make off
With a baron of beef –
He dashed through the back
Of the shop – under surprise attack
From an irate butcher –
Whose expletives gave rise
To scenes of canine ill surprise

I must admit that I
Admired him – he seemed so fit –
This early morning raider
With his barrel chest –
Uncovered – not even a vest –
For this 'four legged' household pest –
Who sprang like a rutting frog
From of a fallen log –
Much maligned – is this heroic butcher's dog

From Viceroy To Hoi-Polloi

There are those who fled the evening dark
On the back of a terse remark
Dashing in a panicked rout – let out
With an accompanying scream – no doubt
But who called them damned?
Force filled their thinking – crammed
It with – ebony gargoyle-like images –
Bringing about the most mindless of scrimmages

Was it an intake of fate or a plate of confusion?
Perhaps simply – a well crafted illusion –
Or a moribund state – brought by a harbinger
Of melancholia – to be heaped on a sad bar binger –
A cringer soaked on whisky and ginger –
Most morose interloper known by all as a whinger
His manic mind set would cause him to flee –
From any real character he dreamed he'd be

So we see these 'august' talkers
Turn and flee – as a group of earnest walkers –
Keenly discussing haversacks
And practical gore-tex macs –
Stout hiking boots with waterproof uppers –
The joys of campfire suppers –
While all the time not ready to admit to doubt
Or that their true character would ever dribble out

These people – unsure – poorly crafted –
Feeling morally above those who honestly grafted –
Can not accept that they are in fact inept –
Believing in a corporate concept
Of class and patronage and British Empire
Brought down by pinko – lefties who conspire –
To cause them harm after dark –
With revolution and a terse remark

Oh To Stop Time

If I could stop time I'd freeze it in May
With spring lambs still at their play –
White hawthorn at drip from the bough –
Tough winter stubble put to the plough.

A spring in sunshine – way past eight –
Lights my way through five barred gate –
To picnic – cushioned in a wild flower lee
Under a gnarled horse chestnut tree.

Time abandoned – standing still
Over the laurels up to Dover's hill –
No watches or clocks striking the hour
Between the Hoo and Broadway Tower.

Along the gallops from an era sadly gone
Through floral meadows lush and long –
Luxuriantly drying out for fodder hay –
Hung with harebells – early rung in May.

A never ending (down hill) soapbox ride –
Of trees climbed with trepidation – bound in pride
Blessed was that time for innocents at play –
Always staged on warm days – still frozen in May

Smoke And Charcoal Grey

How the clouds hold sway –
At the junction of the night
With the weeping day –
Her nimbus rolling forms
Spray the earth's surrounds –
In a dismal low display
Of smoke and charcoal grey

As fate clusters round –
Inquiring how I'm found –
I am called to tell the truth –
I'm in the grey – conjoined
At the scrummage of night
With the weeping day –
Dressed in smoke and grey

My answer is (at best) a gesture
For the place of my rest cure
Is lightless – black of politeness
Where only sightless –
Sonar winged navigators –
Guided by their radar calculators –
Travel unmolested
In this place where I am bested

I bide my time intemperate –
Needy of the time to meditate –
Awash I go with weeping day
To be found at play – away –
In the scrummage of the night –
Where my plight is shown – dressed
In smoke and charcoal grey

By Water, Rail And Road

The company of travelling men
Need to concourse briskly along –
Good roads conveying them
As they build up – into a throng
And as such – would confront all
Who wish to enclose a highway –
That they would always call
A freeman's 'right of gobyway'

As do agree the bedraggled drovers
And – (if knowing) – their charges
Would also allow being driven over –
Canals with horse drawn barges –
Railway tracks with rolling stock
Carrying coal and making steam –
At times choosing to run amok
In livery of maroon and cream

So the roads take perambulating men
Over bridged canal ways – alternate days
With Great Western railways – then
In reverse these hard pad men make way
As they – well organized – return again
Over and under waterways as they gloat
With railways – timetables – restrained
Re-wrote – but not by rail or narrow boat

But by engineers – (who have no time
To gloat) – too busy are they – locked
In to horse power – or what progress grime
Has made each quarter hour – un-mocked
By opposition to mechanical locomotion –
Or it's sticky spats of soot and smoke
Now – that which once caused such commotion –
Is intravenously fed by wealth – industry
Injects into those – who no longer oppose
For they are those – who were once so broke

So stocks and shares triumph over mares –
Now held back for sporting pass-times
While once rough horsemen count what's theirs
In these illuminated – polished rhymes

Ill Founded Gesture

Around the grave-side sombre mourners cluster
As if this death has called them all to muster –
Both family and friends darkly clad –
As though to gesture that they are truly sad
At the passing of this unerring son –
Gone to ground – his life now done

Hands filled with earth are cast to drop
A smatter of contrition on the casket top –
While the jester came dressed as a hooded crow
Who bleats as he retreats across the virgin snow –
His sermon gone unheard – his garb a mere gesture
To the corps – protesting at his oak investiture

The hooded crow gestured in the way he raised his hands
He could – just as easily have been reading marriage banns –
Claiming that he had the ear of God the father
God the son and Holy ghost – rather
Than the truth – that his only unity
Was with wines, beers and spirits –
Which forms such an unholy trinity

Let all those who choose – tell the truth in their overtures
And not fall into that misplaced practice (formed over years)
Has spilled out – without doubt – that all those gone beyond
Were not just perfect but gone glorious, for those who's over fond
Hyperbole warbled in contralto – bass and alto as a vesture –
Misrepresenting truth with such an ill found gesture

My Cheerful Pal Diane

I took a wrong turn into the village hall
Where I wished a good day to one and all
But before I could get on my way
A redheaded temptress persuaded me I should stay
And take part in their next unprofessional play

A play that had an unpronounceable name
And a great deal less in critical acclaim

I regret I can not remain for I've lost my form –
There's no bar and the canned beer is warm –
So let me out before my fans all swarm
And I get soaked in a thunder storm

I cried I'm fed up with fame and the acting game
For I can no longer remember my name

The red headed temptress let down her long hair
A manoeuvre I thought was most unfair –
As she went on to offer me special care
So now I can't get out – for I'm trapped in there

So I say to any young lad – now don't you despair
If you're drawn to thespianism – just be aware
Of women with long red hair and any offers
They make of special care – avoid them
And you'll avoid being trapped anywhere

So now I honour a friend of whom I am fond
For lifting me from my awful despond
Right up to where I now am –
I thank not the Lord but my good pal – Diane

Weary Feet

As I shuffle weary feet
From the tarmacadam street
Along the worn striated track
Of half contoured ruts and tufts
Stretching out to rest on horizon's
Westerly aspect – intact
Broad striped in clover tufts
And barren cuts of bare brown ruts –

The clover's verdant leaves –
Topped by (paled pink ringed) white flowers
Are forced down under the power
Of tamping feet but spring back on
Telescopic stalks that flex
Each time depressed by walkers
Heavily booted feet –
Down on them like an unwanted hex

But my liver and (grubby) white companion
Has no such woes – as weariness –
His cheeriness – he spreads liberally from
Tufted tump to flattened clump –
In hasty dash to catch an imaginary splash
From Lepus Capensis or more likely
In all senses – Cuniculus making such a fuss –
It leaps the wire fences as would Capensis

Which ever he sees as game
Makes game of him – in its superior
Turn of speed – across the standing silage
It has too quick a pace in feet or mileage
So my – (rather sodden) game chaser –
Turns to baser toiletry marking –
Punctuated by his pointless barking

Is – I must admit – though less in flight –
Even more less in grace
As well as all out pace –
But 'muddy coat' is not bowed –
Or in any way cowed nor found wanting –
Though well thrashed – round by round
And so we two inseparables turn
On sum of insect legs without a sound
As we both lope and shuffle homeward bound

Went The Day Badly

As part of the American War of Independence on 19th April 1778 Paul Jones landed an attack force on the shores of Cumberland with orders to destroy any shipping found.

The police spies they were many
And the raiders they were few
So they boarded a tea clipper –
As members – of an aging crew –
For freedom and liberty
They sailed with Paul Jones
And a disturbance of colonial bones –
To Whitehaven they went free
To plunder – across the Irish Sea

Let the boys be called to pray
By end of each long day –
Far from ill timed madness
And – if any charges they be brought –
Proven – putting the boys at bay –
Then they should 'be called upon' – again –
And this time 'be called upon' to pay

Let their apparent madness
Spill forth safely – as would green pus
From bloated boils of sadness
Often in need of leaching
With the minimum of fuss –
For it can not be healed
By a pulpit full of preaching

So these hopes and dreams
Are born to the young protagonists
Who were left forlorn –
For decades – or so it seems –
Mis-managed by a cartel of cartologists
Who sent them on their way
To a Cumbrian bay –
A port of ships and coal barges
Soaked right through at large
In rainy spring – a disappointing cavern
So all mis-givings were washed away –
In the welcome of a local tavern

The Chase

How my dog did stand and stare
Into the chill night air
Perhaps he could see dashing prey
That wasn't really there

But I must follow him
For his wits are far more keen
Than mine – so I chase – with him –
A non existent hare

Across quarry ground beaten bare
Where the chill night air
Had cause to part my hair –
As dog and I stood there –
Out of breath – we no not where

Trench Post Ghosts

Miles of men – special men –
Sieved and sifted – uplifted –
For being specially chosen –
The warp and weft – woven
Into a carpet of infantrymen
Soon to be ripped and torn
Trampled on and badly warn

Oak – elm – chestnut – larch
Booted – taught to march –
No shrivelled stunted dog rose –
Wispy blackthorn or haw –
Simply row upon row of deciduans
Planted to face the iron grey foe
With whom they must maraud –
Out battle – out bloom – outgrow

As young titans – called by Jupiter
To join Neptune – Woden and Mars
Fighting (and dying) tooth and claw
As they –'the more' – slew the more –
In defending those they knew not
In the (aloof untruth) of "hedonistic"war
Brought about by crowned heads
Oblivious to the broader spread

Of felled young growth
All of whom un-knowingly took an oath
To be scythed – part-harvested –
Left un-stooked – unmoved un-barned –
Sorely harmed – de-tuned – de-charmed –
Abandoned to be pressed – crushed –
And metamorphose as Hoosier coal –
Long bled of warmth or breath or soul

Robotic Jazz

Robotic Teachers pre-programmed
To instruct as is their automated way
In the only method that they can –
To a room full of either Dans –
Or of Annes – programmed
With the same soft wear – as
Their instructor's robotic jazz

Pre-recorded – ill afforded
To a pennyworth of children
Unfortunately baptised as Fays –
Bennys or Jennys or Rays
Who were not robotic enough
But too lobotic – or too rough
To be nurtured in traditional jazz

So those dyslexic musketeers
Have (confirmed) – all their worst fears –
For they did not possess musical ears
And their names were in the wrong
So not allowed to join in the song
Now he who didn't – or ever has –
Was made to leave the band of Jazz

But the robotic staff stick close to scales
Teaching those who always fail –
With a method that has been tried
And tested on all those with pride
But those with no ear – were taught by fear –
Singled out – stood or sat at the rear
Where they could not have contact with jazz

Conscience

Who indeed is conscience?
Is he highly principled –
Or simply just a friend?
I wonder does he squander
Or spend wisely – or merely ponder –
On what constitutes 'means to an end'?

If I could find where he lies
I would ask him if he
Would please answer me –
As I am betwixt and between –
For I am so highly principled
In all manners and all means

Finally I would put my request
To him – will he do his best –
In answering my query? –
By saying, "I exist only in the minds
Of troubled people – those
Found tired or distinctly weary"

Yes if only I could find conscience
Free of stuff and nonsense –
I would call to his attention
All those concerns I would like to mention
Such as fairness and diversity –
The exorbitant student fees
Charged on entering university

So conscience if you're out there
Please plague those most unfair –
Such as pompous politicians
Spoilers of old traditions –
Spenders of wealth unwisely
And then 'enter' uncouth people nicely
Forge in them civic pride –
So at least Conscience would be able to say
'That he'd tried'

A Quiet Longing

With a quiet longing I looked
At such a beauty – becoming hooked
Infatuated – slightly inflated
With a yearning – not sated
I was again to be entangled
Painfully flat rolled – mangled

I had hoped against hope for it
Never groped for it –
I almost chocked on it –
The thought of it
Sent me from pillar to post
I ate it on buttered toast
Missed many a Sunday roast
Because of the worry of it –
It caused me to be sick

I was unfit – lost my wits
And half-a-crown – that's 2/6d –
It is made of a strange mix
As round as a brass threepenny bit
I heard bad news of it –
Been falsely accused because of it

It causes much bathing – over long –
Puts on aftershave – too strong –
Given me plenty of shocks
Brings me to put on clean socks –
Has driven me into debt –
Caused me to fret – to forget –
That we haven't as yet actually met

Short Walk Wise Owl

A short walk outside
Where I was waylaid by ice –
About three feet wide
And at the grassy edge – mice
Had hid in hibernation

For so long they had
Been adversely affected –
Lain undetected –
Catching cold so some had cried –
Even more poor mice had died

An owl flew down low
From upon the high elm bough
In his search for his craving –
How those furry boluses were (somehow)
In need of microwaving

For he could not eat
Cold or frozen pellet meat –
And had thought about
Sending them back – in or out
Of the frost wrapped pack

Complaining in hand
Written note – of displeasure
At the hard – bland fuel –
As food and inclement weather
Ta-wit ta-woo – ta-wit ta-woo
What shall I do?
Called the hungry owl

Grace And The Galactipede

I was bound for outer space –
When on my way I saw a familiar face
It was that of my Aunt Grace –
She had left her earthly race
To go full pace – without leaving a trace –
While on the way to her final resting place

Just as each of us salutes the other
She says, "I'm off to see your mother –
How are you and how's your brother?"
I must ask as I don't know one from tother."
"That's because we're so like one another,"
I say, "To differ isn't worth the bother."

It's just then I wished I'd stayed in bed
For I'm alive and she's been a long while dead –
When I mention this she just sees red –
"Such talk shows me you're too well fed."
She screams, "It's meeting you I always dread."
I'm perplexed – for it must be something that I've said

But my mission carries on full speed
To escape – its warp factors that I need –
But I am called upon to succeed
Mr Spock – so I and logic must be agreed –
Before our ship and crew can proceed
To boldly go – way out there in the lead
With a 'state of the art' ship – called a Galactipede
Replacing the aging class – Clingonapede

The captains aboard – all checks are done –
As we're briefed by our number one
I here a voice saying, "Now let's have fun."
It's the ghost of Grace – I am undone –
The Captain's retort was, "Whoever brought that nun
Like spectre aboard this ship must run
Her in – to the mess where she can have gammon –
Pancakes – scrambled eggs – and a currant bun

Finally we set off for space's cosmic Timbuktu
On arrival we disembark and collect the tax's due
By now Grace has painted the planet – day glow blue –
I'm told to put things right before the settler's sue –
I say, "She's a ghost not my relation – what can I do?"
The Captain roars, "She's your problem – so you
Must have her examined by Doctor Drew
And further more – she will be billeted along with you – too

Scarlet Pink

How crass they pose in scarlet pink
With time to kill but not to think –
But enough to drink from stirrup cup
Before they call 'the chase as up' –
View halloo and tally-ho – as they go
In manic dash – to a stand of shedding ash

And how involved are the followers on
Hole stoppers (each and everyone) –
Rushing round on rubber booted feet
To be sure to catch this week's meet –
Hip flasks full though wits are dull
Loosing out (of course) to man on horse
Choosing not to see those who disagree

As worthy of even hot guttural breath
For – too busy are they who seek the death
Of vulpes vulpes – familiaris – canis bait
Known to be devious never running straight –
As could any decent prey be left to stay
On the lie – of a strait and narrow way
So those who would seek fox's blood
Wish it easier – to kill him where he stood

So have more than only their fair chase –
To be able to blood the childlike face
Of a youngster who is not yet sure –
What all this manic action has been for –
But will be true to the view halloo – of
Those crass few who pose in scarlet pink
With time to kill but not to think

Humpty Dumpty

Politically Correct

I often wondered how I'd cope
As a children's story teller –
I think I'd claim I was the feller
Who put Humpty Dumpty
Together again – following a
Slip in horrid - torrential rain –
For I was there when he fell in pain –
After taking a tumble from that wall
In an awful ego shattering fall
But in my tale he is repaired
And his ego spared –
As the King's men just stood and stared
And he – 'the King' – simply
Wrung his hands and glared
While my team of toddlers – very pimply
Helped me out as marshals of the shell –
For I knew my trade – I knew it well

Next I think I'd find the sheep
Belonging to Little Bo Peep –
Or make a carriage for Cinderella
From a discarded martini umbrella –
And when Royal Mail sack Postman Pat –
I'd fill the vacancy with Jess, his black and white cat
I'd service those whistling Clangers
With olive oil and some wire coat hangers

As for skipping – I'd remove the rope
So the children could all better cope –
Reading safety procedures (I must not neglect)
To all taking part – with immediate effect –
And I'd provide pneumatic air beds
To try and allay all those litigation dreads –
Also I'd have a witness – as I aim to direct
All those games – now – deemed 'politically – correct'

'T' Shirt Or Jumper

Lynn could not make up her mind
Weather the day would be cold or fine –
Should she tie up her blonde hair? –
What type of clothes should she ware?
Put on hose and shoes by the pair
Or leave her (tanned) legs bare –
Wear a t-shirt with or without a jumper
A puzzle that was bound to stump her.

"Oh! I don't know," she sighed
"Perhaps if I tried pampering my pride
By dressing in stripes or in check –
Or that blouse that comes up to my neck –
But my tan is gold and the blouse in pink –
Oh God! Please – let me think –
Ah! Yes! I'll wear my prezzy from Aunt Jeanie
My (deliciously) revealing – red bikini".

Once outside – in her hammock she laid –
Cleverly pitched away from to much shade –
Now comfortably strung between pear and cherry tree –
Alone – save for a single (hi-tech) blackberry –
The two of them began to text –
Without a though of what might happen next –
As they sent to an unknown guest
This message – come up and see me
I'm in my hammock –
And (deliciously) revealing – red bikini.

Playing With Fire

I sat up to the Tap Room grate
And settled – for the presentation
Put on by fruit wood fire – warming my desire
For theatrical inspiration –
As small flames of red inception
Played low to the footlights –
While behind – the longer – orange fronds
Danced somewhat higher –
And the yellow castrati
Waved willowy – on the pyre
In their gangly (unsung) plights
And ill-fitting tights

So the apple scent is putrefied
By chemical activity of plot
Leaching sap – on tap
For the sound affects –
On top of cardboard rejects
Commissioned as lighter
For the coming of brighter
Dialogue – choked on smoky fog
At first – coughed by
The damp – star part log –
Who falls foul of flame –
Never now to gain fame

In the final act – when Inspector Ash
Resolves the mishmash
Of evidence – revealing
It was smoke that discoloured
The dun and yellowed ceiling –
But I was to loose the bet –
As my wager turned to sparks
That spit upon the final curtain –
And my rash bet became
More than uncertain
When the culprits were unmasked –
The favoured bet (chain smoked – cork tipped) cigarettes

Warwick Races

With apologies to John Drinkwater, and thanks too, for the inspiration of his poem 'Cotswold Love'.

May skies are over Cotswold
As racing day draws nigh –
The lassies don their fineries
For wagering on horses dashing by
And betting comes in season
When May Day fillies run –
From Longborough out to Warwick
For a day of silken fun.

Their appearance is a marvel
When first the girls arrive
As with determination start to bet
And from the first race thrive
From making wagers
At the totalizer booth
Away form men's inaccuracies
Of tipping – seldom near the truth.

It's little that it matters –
So long as you're alive –
And long past eighteen by May
More rising sixty-five –
When racing comes to Warwick
Under skies of May-time blue –
And Cotswold girls drive away –
Their winnings in their shoe.

Syringa Vulgaris

In Memory of Rachel Pither

A bubbly girl smiled her cheeky smile
As she pulled out a rooted stick – that had
Dwelt in her garden for a while –
Handing it to me with the challenge
Of 'trial by Syringa Vulgaris' –
It's 'expanding into a tree'
Now my task – my obligation –
Which I took on without procrastination
I injected the stick – syringe like –
Into the heavily built up loam
I casually call a border –
Where – now mine – the Syringa Vulgaris
Turns into a lilac candled –
Emerald leaved multi-branched marauder –
Rampant – as was my obligation
To the memory of a girl – now in endless isolation

She took with her – her cheeky smile
Wrapped in jolly bubbles and wild golden hair –
As she had effervesced – so her 'stick'
Now voluminous in livery akin to Olives –
Seemed to do the same – in size and fragrance –
Majestic – it stands for all to see –
But how I wish it was that bubbly girl
Standing in my garden – laughing next to me

Dull Discolouration

Dullness holds this life of mine
Waiting – aching – for the sun that seldom shines
Wrapped (am I) in grey passion –
Calling for a change of colour –
New – re-cut from dull fashion -
As would a jeweller peg set
My facets in dull regret

Sore are my aging needs – though
Contaminated as they are – in throat
Breathing through this gargled glue –
My lunges from air – kept remote –
Kept cold – would be obliged
For a fresher draw on a fare
Intake – with volumes of good fresh air –

So let dullness leave this life
Of aching – for the sun that seldom shines –
Or waiting for the grey wrappings
To fall – as calls for a change of hue
To green – red – white or blue –
In which to set new cut jewels
As set in the crown of my aspirations to be raised to wear –
Over this dull discolouration known as greying hair

Plenty Of Parsimony

Len - Less spent is understood –
As undercut is as good –
The cheapening of the hire
Is – as less logs upon the fire
After all the less logs in hand
The more trees left to stand –
So with my wealth am grateful
Unlike those poor – are fretful.

Bert - But surely as he toils
It's his fat about him spoils –
So he must be worthy hire
As heat is worth the fire –
For the bough that is breezed
Cries fall – is downed – diseased
And then cut in cords
As any (keen edged) axe affords.

Len - I can't give to that
Your vision is a wasteful spat
For coarse ground Flour
Uses less grinding – by the hour
For wholemeal betters whiter bread –
So should be ate instead –
Thus parsimonious use of wealth
Saves stone – while building health.

Bert - No No! – time spent at the inventor's chair
Means machines of less repair –
So more hours winnowing and binding
Without a need for findin'
Mechanical men
To get broke tools to work agen –
So – as feedin' more logs to the fire –
More steam comes to the buyer.

Len - A beast does not over spoil
Fed on graze from wild soil –
An' a baby on poor suck will sulk
As will the one on mother's milk
So less spent is understood
As undercut is just as good.
What say you Ned –
Who's views was the better said?

Bert - Aye – what say you Ned –
Who's views was the better said?

Ned says not a word

Haunted

A spectre came to haunt me
I didn't know his name
He said, "I've been off in search
Of fortune and a modicum of fame –
So let me give you good advice
Don't think that all is right –
As though a mere throw of the dice
Held chance enough to strike a light

There are ghostly activations –
Sad – but nevertheless true –
Which involve the super-natural
And a silk handkerchief in navy blue
Once we and the poltergeists –
Have our victim blamed
He is well chilled and truly iced
So we can have his last remains – reclaimed

I was not easy in his presence –
A shiver ran right through me –
As he told of capers played
On simple folk just for spirit's glee
And if he had once had sympathy
His heart had long ago hardened
To a point where all was about his infamy –
So he had no thought of anyone else being pardoned

"Hallelujah," I cried at last –
"I see how you practice your craft."
Which caused him to look down –
And stare at me – as though I was halfway daft –
"Don't presume to be so clever –
After all – you don't even know my name."
He said – "While you've been wasting time –
I've been off in search of fortune
As well as a modicum of fame."

Water Fall

Written with the July 2007 floods in mind, the author being one of many people flooded.

Though the waterfall was willing –
Due to lack of rain fall
Its flow was slow and weak –
As it slithered and tumbled
Down into the creak –
Where a cascade of mermaids
Sat without feet
And the need of moisture
To avoid defeat – by heat
On the scales of their Piscean tails

So the drought came – a leviathan
Coiled – under the radar – unseen
Below the seasonal 3D screen
Like a thief gone into the night
Before his moonlight skits were seen –
Ghostly – ghoulish – thirst of the foolish –
Unprepared are they for heat radiation –
No plans for (much needed) crop irrigation
Bringing about near starvation

At this moment we floodees mix our emotions –
Remembering that (foul water) '07 commotion
Of our homes – our wits – our chromosomes –
Bringing unbridled damage – repairs – confusion –
So it is – we view drought with consternation
But see flood as monsteration
And would ply for just enough precipitation
To damp the scales of all Piscean tails

Conscientious Moon

Under a crisp full moon
The painter pictured me
By the ebb and flow
Of a turning tide – where he –
Coloured me in swathes
Of charcoal – as lemon bathes
My indiscretions – through soft light
On a well lit summer's night

Perhaps his brush strokes
Are so very broad – they provoke
The shadows to mislead
The rising tide – of nocturnal greed –
But lets slight hand movement
For the good – to be sent
To take well meant donations
And direct them onwards
Towards fine (worthy) aspirations

Or perhaps his brush strokes
Are so very narrow – they revoke
My day's parole – as they delve
Into all my nooks and crannies
Finding items on my shelves
That I had hoped to hide –
Throwing them to the jury bright
Waiting to toss into the light
My indiscretions – opened wide

So he orbits the moon with me
As if he's trying hard to see –
How properly I was made
And could I stand unaided
When taken from the shade –
Could I stand the harsher
Colouring that comes with
Break of day –for glaring
Light illuminates impression
Bumps – and indiscretion lumps
In such a way –
There's nothing left to say
As the moon has had her way

Courtin' Forty Years Ago

I was cortin' a girl from Ilmington
More than forty years ago
In them far off days
When cars an' men was slow –
The cars was so slow
You 'ad t' put yer foot down t' the floor
An' the men was even slower
Cus of all the oggin tackle –
That them wenches wore.

Well I almost picked 'er up
At the place we'd agreed t' meet
Cos me brakes was not so good
An' I overshot – by about a street –
As we set of in the motor
She sez, "I'll take you to
A place – you've never been before."
I said, "There's no need for travellin'
Anywhere 'ere'll do."

Well we'd only gone a mile or so
When she shouts, "You've gone too far."
So I pulls up pretty smartly
An' she takes me in the back seat of the car –
Then sez, "Don't you worry lad
That was just the first."
I said, "Well you'll 'ave to wait a bit
Me dear – 'cos I've
Worked up an awful thirst."

So I takes 'er to the Black Bear
Where – Ol' Doll's stood behind the bar –
An' I rushes down a pint of S.B.A
Where upon Ol' Doll do say,
"Be careful lad – 'cos I know you've just come in the car."
I splutter's into me pint
A wonderin' 'ow she knew –
When she goes on t' say,
"This drinkin' an' a drivin' – it will never do."

Just then the lady youth leader –
A homely little girl –
Sez, "There's a dance on at the football club
An' you promised me – that next time –
You'd give me a comely little whirl."
Well I knowed I was in trouble
So I claimed that I was a fellin' ill
Just as me girl sez come on you –
We're agooin' up t' Bouton 'ill.

Well this was where I met 'er
In the 'orse an' Groom
An' as I sipped a pint o' trophy
I 'ad a awful feeling of – oncomin' doom –
An' that feelin' welled right up
In a way that was like no other
When she finally sez, "Come on you –
I'll take you 'ome t' meet my mother."

Well 'er 'ouse was very clean
A most welcome sort a place
Which was nothin' like the look –
I saw – on 'er mother's face –
She sez, "I 'ope you've bin a treatin'
Me daughter right – attendin' to 'er needs."
I replied that I'd put me coat down
Afor 'er took me in a patch a' weeds.

The ol' dear then sez as 'ow she's tired –
An' leaves – a slammin' the front room door.
Then me girl takes me on the sofa
An' then upon the tiled floor –
Where I tells 'er just 'ow 'ard it is –
An' suggests that we go up stairs instead –
"Certainly not," she cries,
"I don't know you nearly well enough –
To take you to my bed."

Faculties Falter

My faculties falter to a cautious ramble –
Drifting unendingly in slow preamble –
As the softest breeze wings them away
Like dandelion seeds – lost to 'all callings' –
As does the off lead dog – rabbit lifting –
In his hounding – his brisk zigzag drifting

Faculties lost to cybernetic travel –
Beginning to flip flop as they unravel
DNA's double helix – Strand by strand –
No longer perambulating overland
But below a crazy maze of daffodils –
Buried as spring begins to heal all ills

Listening as an angry tide slaps the sand
With it's bilious green sputum (out of hand)
Her waves lift and drop flotsam and jetsam –
Dashed into particles by a refracting spectrum
Cluttered as though the sea had spilt its wealth –
As had my faculties brought on by failing health

So my thoughts lurch – from pillar to post
In absent minded mists – hectoring opaque ghosts
To sweep the fog away and let my faculties be
Free – from their recent moribund promotion –
To take charge of this demonic commotion
And chronic faculties lost in a moronic sea

How pertinent all past knowledge now seems
To my shredded faculties – on line – in eco reams
Relayed in bits and bites – gone into the mesosphere
To be transported through it's rarefied atmosphere –
Re-assembled in the ether to be witlessly defeated
For there is where my faculties will be deleted

Unwanted Dream

I had just had the sack
But felt my luck had changed
When I hitched a ride
On the back of a millionaire machine –
As we strangely ranged – I found
To it's shame – that the machine was so mean
It tossed me back
Like a penn'uth of unwanted bream –
Definitely not a part of my scheme –
Sadly now just an unseemly dream.

Ribald Rabble

A ribald rabble seemed to gabble
Incessantly – their inconsistencies
Of whimsy seemed most clumsy
To the impromptu gathering –
Lathering and blathering –
Because they thought they should be
At a show to which they had –
(somehow) been given passes
Entitling them to have
Free – topped up glasses
Served by a comely gaggle of lassies
Their chassis filled with a range of gasses

An Appearance Of Well-being

Gran – why do you pay so much homage
To windows – knocker and step –
Polishing with such vim and vigour
And a fair indulgence of pep –
When – I'm sure it is painful
The way your knees seem to crack –
Each time you drop down –
With bowed head – and bent back.

You seem to attack this ritual
With vectum and a thick spread of gall –
So please take more ease
When performing this onerous chore –
After all – it seems so un-needy –
For a hailing of grime
Will quickly spatter your efforts –
In the fullness of time.

"Ah! my lad you need to know
That as folk passes by
They're consumed with the need
To figure me out – or at least try –
So I keeps them a guessing –
Then they can only judge by the seeing
Of – well – if not an appearance of wealth
Then – at least a one of 'well being'.

We simulate battle like bespectacled cats –
Circling each other – round to a gloss –
Rubbing over each little misgiving
And that line you never may cross –
Ghosting politely about
In a mild – (though unseemly) chase
That would have been all the better –
For it never having took place.

You see – the holes in your socks
Are never as bad as those nights with no suppers –
As are the holes in your soles as nothing –
If they're cover by well polished uppers –
While all the bounty you comes across 'free'
Is more delicious than any thing bought
So poaching – (like sex) is never a crime –
Cos there's only one crime – and that is getting caught."

Snagged

My fears were snagged upon a thorn
That slowed my stride and length of gait
In the darkest hour – running late
Just before the coming dawn
And shook me into verbosity –
As blood ran down my cheek –
Causing talking in my sleep to leak –
At much letting of quality
From my complicated nightmare –
So had found no enlightenment there

It was then the brier crept into attack
Sending elongated tendrils –
Be-throned and self willed
Into a knot tied around my back
To cause much discomfort at the scratches
By now running as if freed –
Seeming licensed to drip and bleed –
Each jagged pierce – a part of sore patches –
Rashes strewn about my body – damaged
By thorny briars as they march on – unmanaged

How – I asked myself – did black thorns
Enter my twilight world of charcoal nights
And the pitch black of even darker sights
Infested with black demons – their horns
Protruding into my mind's inner space
Then it comes to me – thorns are Seimans
Missiles with warhead black demons
That – first compressed – explode – apace
Making their murky way in to hide
And practice mayhem – (perniciously) – inside

How similar are thorn poxed briers –
To the devil's – black imp (polished) liars
(In the damage and discomfort that they cause) –
With their invasion of the ailing mind – their claws
Opening wounds – left to fester – dark thoughts
Like pussious – course – deep rooted warts –
Gaining hold on fragile sanity – dug in
Planted on the skin like sockets put there to plug in
Viral main lines of antimatter to creep
Around the brain when host is caught in fractious sleep

Silence

A silence held my dread
Transfixed me deep inside my head
Muted was my defence –
In scarlet – such an intense
Hue – causing my face and neck –
To thicken with blood vessel bark –
And ruby face – equally stark

I was now being held
In a vice of discord – bolt and weld
Spun in elliptical orbits –
Centrifuging my plaudits –
So clapping and adenoidal diatribe
Were specked with a metallic rash –
Lit by a parsec lightening flash

Then the long night came
To cover me with a mulch of tree bark –
Ash sparks lighting the dark
As though from electrodes
Clean – conductive – sparring with anodes –
Diodes and cathodes standing fast to do battle
One with another – causing a deathly rattle

Spilt slumber followed –
A torpor of nightmares – gargoyled stares –
Dense sleep hollowed
No longer holding worldly cares
Disturbed by electrical storms of agitation –
Given off by broken electronic gadgetation
Yet to be bestowed with accreditation

A silence caused by item
Of electronic goods that would – but frighten
All – with their jolting
And lack of sparks for halting
Their machining – their whirring and rotating –
Computing – compilating – printing – annotating
Explaining – highlighting – mailing – connotating –
Strangulation – or death in crimson violence
Certain to end on time – in silence

Gone is the roistering of the shipyards
The foundries and rolling mills
With their ethical hubbub
A cure for all ills

Just Observed

Will I be perturbed?
Or undisturbed
At the thought of
My stubborn pride
Or my missing bride –

The girl who cried
I said I would – but I lied
I want no more to do with you –
Yes it's true

Just as my pride
Took a fall from a barnyard wall
My cries mixed in with
Horse dung flies –

So I am perturbed
And most disturbed
At my lack of success –
My self made mess
My old age arthritic distress
Not seen – but just observed

Marbled Ground

High above the marbled ground
At stall – the peregrine there watched –
Below winged the "grey head" fieldfare
Surveying arable tilth all around
Until he spots an incandescent hare –
As above the falcon circles – to no sound –
With expectation of a morning rare
Breakfasting – of (chilled bone) adolescent fare

The young hare – overheating
In his rash "long striding" dash
Has a high – runway greeting
From the aerial tiercel crash –
For rapid talons dig deep – cling
True – as quarry and hunter
Now as one – resume their wing –
So – no second chance for (daring) hareling

The fieldfare and Redwing
Can only stare at the fate of leveret hare –
Then resume their needy repast
Of hedgerow berries and other juicy fare
Such as earth bound invertebrates
Now unfrozen by the warmer winter day
Repast – for they must consume enough
For returning migration – to Norway – by the end of May

Cold Winter Bed

So winter's ermine cloak falls – as bitter cover
Over rich – chocolate impasto loam –
Thorn infested hedge – and trees above her
Fresh cropped (matting) home –
Lodgings for worms and viral nematodes
Called to hibernation as monks might
Be – to pray in (cell like) sparse abodes
Without tuck – or warmth – or fickle light

Hearing the sounds that reverberate around –
Of coughing throats and sneezing noses –
From those who turn the ground
Digging – planting and mulching roses –
De-mossing – compost tossing –
Servicing secateurs with carborundum stone
For pruning and training leaders – crossing
Ribbed arch – so is fruit wood tunnel grown

Waiting for the crystallized – amalgam grit fall
Of lacy hexagons and roundels –
Reinforcing the seasons freezing maul –
Joining in with other winter scoundrels –
Spiked and fronded round and wanded –
These bleached ballerinas pirouette
Like free spinning hexettes – soon bonded
As woven – warming – Wilton Plaquet

Finally all is enveloped by the heaviest of dews
Within its – echo deadening – clinically
Bleaching – far reaching call on distant views –
At first – seemingly healing – but cynically –
Teasing – freezing all life's soak
To this scene – an unspoken tapestry of folk law –
Barbaric in its rustic woven cloak –
Expounded and expanded over a rash of spoken gore

So all is freezing – (nothings easing) – to some – most pleasing –
This esplanade of cotton wool drifts and spills –
Soon utilized – this horticultural land – appeasing
A spree of toboggan – skate and skiing thrills
Gardening pledges gone with privet hedges
As all is as one – now that snow has come –
To all man's good intentions – crumbling under sledges
And surrendering to the battle ice has finally won

A Miser's Walk

A miser walked around the cost –
When offered a replacement
Fore something that he'd lost –
It was hard to understand
His parsimony of reasoning –
Being spread with so much
Caustic seasoning –
As if shaken from a worn and
Dented cruet (so vigorously) –
It started everybody sneezing

So aggressive was the discharge
Expelled from this parsimony's nose –
It contaminated an angel's hose
And caused a seraphim and
Cherubim to come to blows –
Bringing the miser cause
To share his many and varied woes –
Such as snoring in his sleep –
Waking late for the rummage sale
And so missing a chance – through doze
Of replacing his 'hand-me-down' old clothes

So mean he was – came chatter's buzz –
That he refused a life saving operation –
One of the transplanted organ type –
Until he was satisfied any complication
That arises – would be at public expense
For he was concerned that if he was contused
His funeral insurance might be abused
By his after death remains being sued –
So paranoid was he – so it was said
He'd be careful not to die in bed
So his estate would not be sued for any pending laundry dues

Guarding The Apple

Dappled in shafts of sunlight
And early morning shade –
The green picket fence
Of keen young daffodils
Threw protection around –
The apples grafted might

As yet unhatted – barren –
As tender carrion –
For the mower blades
And slug and snail raids –
Narcissus spandrels –
Clean – green – seen –
As light absorbing candles

There – in spite of winters
Frozen vapour hoards –
Spreading a fungus
Of frozen white spores –
Collectively know as hoar –
Taken – by lengthening days
Pouring a sunlit praise –
In patterned spring time dapple –
Over guardians of the apple

Bespoke Smoke

I was called by an old rocker to cast
My mind – A hard walk – far into my past
Where the decades fall away at pace –
Revealing a lack of thought a lack of grace
From those like me who act in haste –
Were born across the cobbler's last
Exchanging hob nail boots
For poppy shoots
And balding tyres – rabbit wires –
For chemical smokes
Made to measure suits –
Almost tailored – replaced by
Controlled substances – almost bespoke

Super imposed music – re-hashed
From men who once smashed
Their uncouth way
Into 'taped play' of the musical 'harvesters hay' –
Now CD – DVD's discharge gargling throats –
Forming gutterel gloats –
Straining to recall through a haze
Filled cocaine milled maze –
Once sharp – now flat –
Brought low to the blues of that
Mind – thick with yesterday's porridge
Nasal passages 'cut' with
A hybrid of Saxifrage and pale Borage
All high from a smack attack –
If only I could I would go back

Note:
Harvesters hay = successes of the sixties
pop music – fashion – electrical goods

Pre-recorded Saviour

I saw the sun was too low in the sky
So I called up my guardian angel
To ask him why –
But a machine answered –
It's because of your cancer
So don't bother calling again –
We hate to hear an old man cry

So I waited till the sun was high
And once again I thought I'd try –
To call upon my afore mentioned angel –
Firstly to see if he was at work
And if so did he have a quirk
For answer phones –
Mobile homes –garden gnomes
And avoiding his client's moans

This time the phone said I was in a queue
With Vivaldi and his seasons
For no logical reason –
Than someone wanted me there –
It wouldn't be more than a couple of minutes
For the voice seemed to know I was nearing
The limits of my despair – what with being
Used for training purposes – it said the same –
For my mother's maiden name

I spoke to Mat (from Katmandu)
Who used to work in Timbuktu
Besides a week or two down in Peru –
But the travelling he found was too much –
He said he needed to be a great deal nearer
So that he could keep in touch.
He then disclosed he got the job unopposed –
But he must resign his post in haste
And re-apply
As a group for 'free and fair' elections
Have taken up the case –

They told him to make his application twice
And if he got the job in front of himself –
Well now – that would be nice –
I said I was pleased to hear he was being harassed
As I was (by now) somewhat brassed –
And – if he saw my angel again – tell him
I would rather live on my best behaviour –
Than go on with him – as my pre-recorded saviour

Not First Not Last

Not the first
To make an entry
By means of
Natural birth.
Nor first to cry
Or try
To reason why –
There could be doubt about
Creation –
As though it was
All imagination
Set out for us to view –
Unknowing –
That the chosen one
Is overdue.

Not last
To have less future
Than had past –
Having lived
Three score years
And ten
As do many men.
Now lain –
Inactive brain –
No more need to train –
Cadaver
Without laughter
On the path
To
The hereafter.

Orange And Gold

Hallucinating while receiving acupuncture

The needles find their channels
From the head down to the ankles –
Where orange blood wept out
Dripping on to the golden mouse –
Who crept about the house –
Across the parquet floor
In search of the 'up step' door.

As quickly as it came – the blood
Congealed its self-effacing flood
Withdrawing from the golden mouse
Like fire from the water douse –
Colour coded it did rescind –
Blown about on imaginary wind

To be assayed as unafraid –
Hallmarked – was the mouse betrayed
As fools gold – left unsold
Abandoned to the thoughtless cold –
That froze the mandarin blood
Stemming the creeping citrus flood –
Leaving those sharper aches
As unsolved yin and yang mistakes

How much were these visions –
Brought by medicine transitions –
Ones diagnosed as anorexic
Creating symptoms apoplectic –
As distance spread in anticipation –
From eye to brain – as contamination –
In the form of a citric hallucination

Spirit Of The Market

Spirits came from the merry market
As the traders paid – unaware
Of deals made at the very parquetry –
The centre of the trading square –
Of young tegs pens and drinking dens

All silver transactions now finalized
By well bred men and their scandlings
Who – by duplicity –bind their prized
Stock – to a scoundrels heavy handlings

So the spirit moved from market pens
To the inside of the drinking dens
Where all were welcomed to take
A break and sate for hungers sake

Spirit quickly out – to the vibrant square
To resume activities of the market there –
Auctioneer calling out for opening bids
From reticent dealers 'stood off' pen grids

Keepers of spring lambs and lame sheep
A chorus or two of quarrelsome geese
Calves just half grown –ready to leap
A cart of pullets – near to lay – are cheep

Surrounded by a bound of scrounging
Pups all too similar to a call – of lounging
Lurcher types lean and low of position –
Course of discord – crass of disposition

So is the craze joined – by whooping boys
Taking a truant day and bringing noise –
These uncosseted 'colts' there for the hiring –
Bold in uncensored belief of never tiring

Let the aging crone (of ragged garb) squawk
Down trumpetous nose – curled as a hawk
Would – from fair distance of the corporation –
Bedecked as though attendant on a coronation

So all classes have their raucous aspirations –
Though few will have gained core vibrations –
Telling them they can have due deliberations –
Believing they are truly – 'great men' of nations

Unwelcome Sleuth

The sleuth of enmity
Fell short – slipping
Into a mire of jealousy –
While trying to drown the sound
Of pleasantries – played
Out by joyful souls
On violins – as well as
Jaunty flings danced to
Flutes and mandolins
And rare acoustic strings

Antagonism was his aim –
As at the doors of all and sundry
He tried to lay the blame –
'I caught you out'
He is known to shout –
Making merry –
Drinking juice from
Distilled fruit and berry

But we crowd him out -
Send him scurrying
From our thresholds
Held by a community of unity –
We send him slipping into
The gripping mire
Of unpleasantries – wire
Barbed around unplayed flutes –
Drug inflicted flings
And music from lutes
And mandolins – tuneless
Without the music of their strings

Long Term Sick

Re-arranged appointments –
From Tuesday to Thursday –
Nine to eleven –
From February to as far off as May.
My diary is suffering from bouts
Of blotched crossings out.

A life now – inked in
To dated blank pages –
Flat – near illegible scribbles –
And entered in haphazard stages –
A reflection of life's wealth
As valued by our national Health.

Good people – pressed for time
In their dash to save cash –
Efficiency rushed in quick consultations
Diagnosing shingles as just a bad rash –
And telephone conversations
Set up – to placate overwrought patients.

Re-arranged appointments
From this Monday to sometime next year
Eight in the morning put back to three thirty –
But there is nothing to fear –
E.coli has simply been eradicated
And all super bugs are officially post-dated –
So don't worry about catching infection –
For with us – there's now no connection
Because these germs won't start to roam –
Till long after you've gone home.

A life re-arranged around medical strife –
Of yet again – cancelled appointments –
Bookings for holistic therapies
To have massaged away – disappointments
Received in messages that I feel conveyed –
He's lingered too long – welcome outstayed.

Inconvenient Big Toe

How far can I go?
With these old wooden crutches –
Nowadays I'm so slow
My walking's quite poor you know –
Since braking my big toe

So I have been limited
By lack of reasonable motive force –
Feeling Intimidated
By the principle of leavers – simulated –
Inundated – complicated –

By damage inflicted
To my stress fractured phalanges –
Movement restricted
By plaster – my toe now constricted –
And I've grown addicted

To morphine patches –
Stuck on in such a haphazard manner
That – firstly catches
Pain – and once its helix matches –
The dull ache it dispatches

I'm still too slow
With these old wooden crutches –
I'm not even fit to row –
So now Its taxis everywhere I go –
Since clumsily braking – my big toe

Eilean Arainn

I heard two clouds in whispered conversation
As they morphed into a ring around Goat Fell
Let us unlock this brave terrain by invitation –
To those hardy zoologists bobbing on the swell –
Disturbed by the thrash – out of the Sound of Bute
Called 'nothing but a cut' to steaming Waverly
Passing Ailsa Craig – righteously – rigged to suit –
Making Brodick quay for tea –seaming verily

Disgorged by steel modernity – modesty accepted
Wisely – from Mullach Mor – a flit to Killbrannon –
Dancing such distance along the string – proofed
Looks at Peregrines – Ptarmigan by Bennecarrigan –
Take to the sea by kayak – let sun and stretch tone
The skin – tune latissimi dorsi and deltoid round
As far as reason – then to tented home – to moan –
Till Corrie lounge tunes us in to a ceilidh sound

So the red grouse reluctantly serve their use –
While red squirrels abound – barred from strop
Or ball or barrel – pleased at debarment truce –
So – sail in the woodland head – spread as crop
Of tourist must – scurrying to lead almost a fray
Of enthusiasm – to hide in the King's cave
Where I heard the waves in conversation – spray
Those near enough – to hear enough – called brave

So let conversation softly tap on the Goat's hat
Her granite leaders – sharp backed – Neanderthals –
Spread above Machrie's hexagon of stone éclat –
Where bare mornings – washed by thunder spells –
Are soon dressed in a sunshine cloth of yellow
As many of Arran's raptors soar above waterfalls
Rolling south – as tenants of rough – once of mellow
Disposition can be punctuated by the earnest calls
Of Golden Eagles prey – warning of finality aspray –
While intent on living past the ending day

Ballad Of War

Now Tommy's gone from off the farm
To the battle fields of France
Where – he says – there are pubs and clubs
And halls for them to dance.
The weather's fine – the music's grand
And the girls are full of charm
So Mother dear – please have no fear –
For there's no way – that we will come to harm .

Through Hell's blackening umbrella's
Spread wildly overhead –
More valedictory ordinance flies
To spatter whole lengths of defences
With a (mass produced) crescendo of death
Cascading from Flanders – now leaden skies.

While Tommy's gone from off the farm
To those trenches dug in France
Where – he says – he lies by a limbless corpse
As he wakens in a blood stained trance.
The birds are gone and the mud's come on
And the rats are everywhere
So Mother dear – let it be clear
That we are well and thriving here.

Delicate – not yet shaving – voluntary men
Spread as adolescent porcelain –
Morosely fire cracked – to craze –
Most to crumble – flicker out
As either blown by their own bugle call
To ashen death – or left in fitful daze.

Our Tommy's gone from off the farm
To the killing fields of France
Where – he says – he's shot another Hun
Who's arms were gone – he never stood a chance –
Oh! those Germans are some brutes to us
Not like ordinary men –
They seem to have a need to kill –
Much as we have a need – of killing them.

No they are not like ordinary men –
Seeming to have a need to kill –
Much as we have a need of killing them
Yes a manic – a satanic – need of killing them

Maidly Care

"Let me help," she says politely,
"Pull you from the deep –
Let me help you nightly –
In your calculus of sheep."
Let me sift through
Each strand of brittle hair –
Let me lend a helping hand
To shake the floss
From your cloth of grim despair."

"I can sit quietly –while you reflect
Or leave you while you dwell –
And at your express request –
Can sing to you and shall.
I can sing a lullaby
To help to sooth you –
Run my fingers cross your brow
And try to smooth – too
Your troubled laughter lines –
Now creased by harassment of day –
Let me unfreeze your ruddy skin
And wash your frown away."

"Let me relate to you a joyful tale
Or caress your senses with a poem
From Robert Frost – or our lost
Brother – Wilfred Owen.
Or let me bubble hot a bowl of broth
And feed through your pustled lips
Slowly – not in scalding sips –
To scorch – like (too near candle) on the moth.
I would willingly set down the bowl
And curl – intertwined
About your heart and mortal soul".

I speak thus – "I care much for your grief –
But you must distance now from death – the thief –
For where I go you can not follow
Now my heart is broke and my soul tolls hollow".

Salute To Ol' Totty

Ol' Totty went t' Scuttlebrook in the fancy dress
'e played a push-biker who 'ad crashed
An' was in a helluva mess –
But 'e won fust prize –
Proof as 'e is a mon who is still very wise –
Well! y' could see it in 'is eyes

They Butty Girls were there
All done up as royalty – an' what a merry lot
But I couldn't tell which Butty girl was what –
Then Livi – well – she was took short
A leavin' a message on 'er phone
Sayin' I've 'ad t' dash – t' find a proper thrown

Well they 'ad all escaped from Yubberton
Gone in Search' of a bit o' fun –
They was settled on a cart
When there was a raspin' noise so loud
I thought the cart 'ad come apart –
Still it seemed t' please the crowd

Nan got fancy dressed an' took part agen –
She's bin a doin' it since I don't know when –
'er's always controversial – (I 'ad t' look that up)
While I was doin' that – they gev Nan a special cup
When I was told – I couldn't believe me ears –
That Nan 'ad bin at it – for nigh on 400 years

There was a surgeon there
An' a woman who seemed in gret despair –
She said I should 'ave gone to Spec Savers
Instead of to see dodgy Dr Wavers –
Well I'd wondered to what Tooloo now aspired –
For it's near a year since 'e retired

The history Girls 'ad found a new twist –
They'd dressed up – on a truck – as the livin' whist
But didn't know where they could park it –
Shame on the wit who shouted 'Stratford market'
They played with giant cards the size of pavers
Perhaps it was them – as should 'ave gone to Spec Savers

The Volunteer didn't get very far
With their new barmaids on a mobile bar –
Bring back Laura – Sarah and Di sez I
They was a gret deal easier on the eye
A word of advice boys – so now listen 'ere –
Next year – while parked up – sell some of the beer

When all 'ad finished Livi put the Butty tractor's nose bag on
Settling it in the paddock when all the oats were gone –
Then the girls quaffed some home made beer
With those friendly barmaids from the Volunteer –
Now all that was left to do for Livi – Fi and Alice
Was to find their way 'ome – to the 'Butty palace'

Authority Of Elements

How close the storm
Looms over me
I feel it's aggressive
Energy – drowning me
As I'm left to stem the tide –
Nowhere to hide –
Caught where I stand
On shifting sand –

A day's walk from anywhere
Without a friend –
No thoughts or tools
On which I can depend –
It seems that movement
Has me condemned –
Breath and brawn hemmed
In – I myself fair clemmed

But air and oxygen
Put me in hope's box again
With life's coxswain
Pulling me above the
Thrashing sea to stand on land
I am sure – called shore
Wild cliffs and grassy moor
No more – but concrete
Wharf and esplanade

Amongst The Buddleias

I was sure that I had seen her
As I looked and looked again
There – quick step dancing –
Was a splendid lady wren –
Preening amid the top growth –
Of vegetation sprawl – spreading
Over – from my neighbours garden wall

Such a rare sight was she
I began to hope – even pray –
That this was her start anew
And she would choose to stay –
Even nest there in amongst
The buddleia and the broom –
Parading for me each morning
And for many an afternoon

I was so impressed by her –
Her dull dun plumage seems
To be so well tended – I'd swear
She was of polished elm as she gleams –
Causing me such excitement – I've
Decided in order for her to stay
I'll hold back any blade from that bush –
For it might drive my wren away

Crystal Flakes

Snowflakes swirled towards me
Like a whitewashed swarm of bees
Dashed against various dormant trees –
Becoming unique insect casualties
Building on their own cold – hard –
Barron honey combs – beneath
A parade of translucent shards
Dangling as would mongol swords

The attack was quite ferocious
With bad behaviour – most atrocious –
Mindless breaking down of power lines
Putting back most traveler's destination times –
Being rolled to and fro (by traffic) into ice
As they are re-routed without choice
To slip and slide –without a voice
While trapped by cold snap's winter vice

But in time the swarm was grounded
Though rumours of a thaw – unfounded –
Let the swarm arrived as crystal flakes
To set like icing spread on cakes –
Badly In need of candles heating tricks
Or better still – by sunlit pyrotechnics –
But for now it refuses to get up and go –
Lying around as shapeless piles of brindle snow

Those flakes that whirled across the night
And curled between the beams of moon's new light
Have now been contained without excmpliture
Are turned to a marinade by rise in temperature –
No longer carpeting roads and roofs
But turning byways to mud – with cloven hooves –
Churned to an unpalatable freezing slush
That doggedly lies beneath the hawthorn bush

Such a volume of snow gives no favours
(As in its grip) a whole country slavers –
Pitter pattering through the crumbling mire –
Vainly in search of a rainbow choir
Who would take up their books and sing
A madrigal to crocus in an early spring –
So leading us from this wake of swirling flakes
Through to a spring – that early brakes

Remembrance

A broad mind can find
Thought chaffing –
While self effacing –
Scouring their kind

That brittle tread
Of men long dead
Taken at the cusp
Of military lust

Approach my door
Marching to a band
Of one handed roars
Playing military lore

They and their souls –
(Underground moles)
Call for recognition
Of postmortem position

No waving flags
Shot to filthy rags
Lofted by lean men
Let breath again

All citations desisted
No medals struck
Just (as within the muck)
They had once existed

Trevor's Retirement

Comments made on the retirement of Trevor Wosket,
Campden Fireman

I remember the day he started –
Of course he was different then
With a mop of thick black curls
And weighting twelve stone ten –
He said I am a very fit man
With the reactions of a cat
And I played football every week –
Till age and marriage changed all that.

Their kids came quickly once they'd moved,
Which was quite enough for Jen
"We'd better stop at two," she said,
Or we might have to move again.
Well their kids were quite inquisitive
And made old Trevor laugh
The time they asked, "Who is that bloke
In Mummy's wedding photograph."

I spoke to Des the other day,
'e said, "Trevor's seen some sense at last.
I know he's done well "up there"
But it's about time he put it in the past."
I always admired how calm Trev stayed
In the face of all commotion
And the skilful way 'e managed to avoid
All those offers of promotion."

He was nearly as good as me
Though not at mowing grass –
Too busy with Ol' Des on windows,
Which reminds me – I need more ten ounce glass."

Well Trev! I liked the way you chose to go
I liked the way you went.
By choosing a time to suit yourself –
At a time before you were completely spent.
I think you've shown good judgement
I think you've boxed real clever,
And I'd like to say, my time served with you –
(Especially in the Volunteer) – has been a real pleasure.

Good Health Has Passed Me By

Good health has passed me by
As I dream by the candle that flickers –
Of garden bonfires, picnicers and
Taking heed of perennial pickers –
Some local – some itinerant –
Here for the harvest of soft fruits
Pulses – hay – and potato yields –
Green vegetables sat in half pots
Waiting for transport from shorn fields

Horses' hooves and iron tyres
Make merry with the dawn –
Tapered churns bring ambrosia
By milk float – horse drawn –
On un-metalled roads – old tracks –
Where tufted grazing parts wheel ruts –
Contouring about below hedge-rows
Punctuated with shedders of nuts –

But I have seen none of them –
As still I sleep without recourse
To merriment – no music brushes
My cold cheek – still awaiting the force
Of betterment – brought by oxygen
Coursing blood – while harvests turn
Another good barn of mainstay crops
And full stacked hearth of logs to burn

Puppies grow – chase the stones we throw –
Slip the lead and course rabbit's scuts
Pedigrees and those with fleas (do as they please)
Whether run to hyperbole or just tut tuts –
Seen not by me – for I am with Sean –
Gone to sea where wash comes over me
No quiet pints – no quaint good nights –
Or dawn's chorus – with 'first light' reverie

Or walking along the wool sack way –
Where a covey of partridge scurry
In their haste to gain flight –
Give such a release of energy as they hurry –
But the stiff laced boots that 'put them up'
Mottled of a dew dulled shine –
Are on other feet – strident as the morning air –
That refreshes other lungs – not mine

July Aspect

A flight of swifts came in drifts
Locating – with high pitched song –
Each the other winged invader –
Swarming across the blue July
Aspect – pitching and yawing –
steepling into the azure high –

While we – in our length and breadth
Peopling – can only stand by –
Each a mere promenader
Without a third dimension
To allow us such overseeing
As that of this mercurial wing master

So the company of swifts lay claim
To their high altitude feeding grounds
While thrush and dunnock
Hop step and bounce around
Scavenging along the walkway rails
On windfalls worms and snails

Seeming almost earthbound –
Until the silent cat mistakenly
Makes a rustling sound –
Causing an emergency chattering
Of 'speckled hopper' flights
Taken to avoid a feline battering

While swift swoops – rises – dipping – crying
In his vying for repast
Of winging insects – not fast enough
To evade the swirling cuff
Of confidence worn by
This sharp Nimrod of the sky –
Dominant across this aspect of July

Come The Day

A sadness came to stay
Drawn about my face –
Darkening my frown lines –
Sitting in every place
Of depth – each nook –
Each cranny – letting
Tears brook
Down my hollow
Cheeks – sagging –
Worn and lagging
Far off in youthful play –
Chanting –"Come the day –
Come the day."
All verdant sedges
Waving to cousin grasses –
And resplendent hedges

Azure and pure skies
Now demised –
Compromised by
Constant grey –
Oh! come the day
Come the peaceful day

Jugs And Mugs

A collection of jugs hung from the shelf
Some used for visitors – others for myself –
But there is little or no crockery
To serve up carrots peas and broccoli
And not a sharp knife for carving
Any meat for the starving –
So I cancel my ill fated distribution of grub
By ringing round all my guests from the pub

Some of them seemed quite pleased
While others seemed somewhat peeved –
Saying it was my rare invitations
That caused stress to their patience –
For they had canceled something better
On receiving my invitation letter –

So I tell them that too much haste
Will invariably ruin any meals taste
Meanwhile those guests – who were pleased –
At the treatment they had received
Where busy running up my bar bill
By the sounds of that old fashioned till –
It's bleepings and squeakings call out aloud
That those who were pleased – were quite a large crowd
For when my bill was presented for my contemplation
I was forced to declare my own financial – liquidation

Shimmering Earth

It's brown and more shades of brown I must resist
In their chocolate darkness absorbed by
Plough blades turning – furrows brought to list
In tight rolls of shimmering soil – kept dry
Broken – charcoal aerated by the earthworm
From bare to barren as drought leaches graze
Left as tinder waiting for a fire storm
To set umber catastrophes – ablaze

Now spring brings the planting of the wheat corn
In tilth of sand and leaf mould's darkened loam
Fertilized by phosphates and powdered horn
Browns and reds of blood and bone – dried of foam
For improved growth after crop rotation
Urged to thrive by harvest time rogation

Absent Minded

A fresh breeze took my mind
To a place that I could never find –
A place in which I would pay to stay –
Where all my thoughts were chronicled
And neatly filed away

Lost upon some dusty racks –
Deep in the archive bowels of hope –
My plans and schemes are packed –
And without them I shall barely
Manage (in my frailty) – to cope

For I am in the autumn of my years
Decanted of my bygone youth – new fears
Have taken favour – of ganglions transmitting
Arthritic pain – saying you have nothing
Left to lose and little left to gain

So it's said – that my aging empty head
Will be filled with eccentricities or senile dread
But I laugh as my fears turn to running sand –
For now I have no room to understand
So talk of doom is banned

Unceremoniously and offhandedly
From the shelves of common practice
Where I believe my final act of contract is –
'Will-like' – as a paper of candid invalidity
Or (more likely) aging stupidity

Though empty headed – I am inclined to say
Helped by a westerly breeze I'm sure I will find
The unknown whereabouts of my forgotten mind
For thoughts – once spread in clumsy disarray –
Are (by now) – filed and neatly packed away.

Important Friendships

All important friendships are made
At a time of need – afraid
They will not last – good friend
Held well while the sun shone
Now rejected – memories gone –
About their travels – not made
Amends – frayed of ends

Unmeasured – un-kempt – unseen
Lost in the thought
Of what might have been –
As with letters written –
Wound tight – screwed up –
Finally discarded –
Un-posted – gone unrewarded –

Though postage could be
Well afforded – so to the church –
That took my breath in promises
Made for me – sees parents gone
God parents – who no longer live on –
What a comfort they once were

Let right choose to bring them
Back again – with those
Familiar words I wish to hear
Within my ears – conquering
Latent fears – as their heads appear –
Called by demons to lie near –
To lie here – to cost dear –
Breed fear – year on year –
Without those familiar words
Of important friendships – I dreamt were near

Apple Christening

There was a casualness about July
On St Swithin's morning – letting fly
As it allowed the clouds to dapple
Harvest growth – ridge and furrow –
Lapwing's nest and rabbit burrow –
And over orchards of fruiting apple

Among we 'seniors' there are folk
Who can recall the 'rhyme of soak –
Of rain fall – of apple christening
Put squarely on the shoulders of St Swithin –
There would be rain at least within
Forty days and nights and listening

To it's pitter patter while drizzling –
Or to downpour or simple mizzling –
Punctuating this tenth centaury spat –
Till the sun arrives – turning the flow
To refreshing mist in summer blow
Just enough to take off a bishop's hat

So the legend of this religious squall
Is known for christening apples all –
By the hand of Swithun from heaven
Between the sunlight and the shade
His saintly – baptismal cross is made
From the rolling downs as far as Devon

So it was that this bishop of Winchester
Preached of God and damp sou'wester
Over apples of Jonathan and cats head –
Granny Smith – pippin and braeburn –
Russets and names we have yet to learn
All casually caught in his water shed

Let it not rain on St Swithin's play
Known to us as the fifteenth of July
So let us never see this date pass by
Without praying for a cloudless sky
And fair weather like we had last May
Spread over Apple Christening day

Integrity

Integrity – an inner force –
Or merely born out of remorse? –
Whichever –
A quiet gathering of righteousness
And experience – drawn to redress
Malevolence –
And deviant malpractice –
While reassuring with benevolence.

Integrity – born from trust
Or just grown like mould on a crust?
Seemingly
Only as an outer coating
Of truth cloaking – an innards of gloating.
Frippery
Now holds sway – way
Beyond the innocence of parlour trickery.

Integrity – can not be bought
Or caught
Though there are those – who conceive
A plot for their fellows – whom they would deceive
With well practised chicanery –
Melodrama –
Secret evidence given in camera –
Rooms blacked of view from any ensuing drama

Integrity – a rare commodity –
Unseen
But used by a fine majority
To bring to book those ingrates in their pajority
To set the records straight –celebrate
A triumph
Of all that we hold good
Over those who are determined to sling mud
But never to give blood

Worth The Harvest

As the spliffs and tapers blaze
Sending all into a lasting haze –
With wayward stiffs – drawn
In to temptations maze –
Enough to hear plantation's
Praise – worth the harvest
Through substance' glaze

So it is we seek out – the daze
Of addicts who have left those ways –
Though wan and warn
They are in recovery faze –
To keep concentration's
Strays – to help divest
Habits (that on substance) graze

Hope of recovery plays
Before the resolute phase –
(Pubescent recovery) is lashed with scorn –
So cravings bleed – so pumping sprays
Crimson contaminant about – consternation
Plays all – to invest –
(As the spliffs and tapers blaze)
In banning this corrupted substance craze

The 'Boat House'

"Slippery." She said –
And slippery it was – the path that lead
Down to the beach –
Just a shortish reach to the demanding
Bleach of froth –
Slapping the sand – as if reprimanding
Those too near
As tho' teaching paddlers tidal etiquette
About getting wet

"Here." She said –
Just here is where it was – that dinghy
That upturned –
'Sea-shed' – boyhood den that spurned
Door or floor
A 'lair' – where we adventurers earned
Our water spurs
In this heaven sent bark – clinker built

House on silt
"An age ago." She said
An age ago I know too well I sighed
Inwardly – as if to hide
Those pangs of need for famished pride
Lost on an adult tide
Washed out by eddying responsibility
Though I always tried
To stay awash with youthful humility
Sadly now put aside

"That hull." She said –
That hull once had been a castle keep –
A dry place to sleep
When we stood guard – under orders –
Against marauders –
Once it was a far distant foreign gaol –
Beached blue whale –
Grounded man o' war lost in a gale
Caught without sail

"Attacked." She said –
Attacked as chieftain's hut – hacked –
Plundered sacked –
Mountain top complete with flag on –
Fiery winged dragon
Kidnapped princess – with gag on
Rescued by Ron –
Who stole a kiss later on – for a lark –
All these dreams played out on 'our'
Magic – upturned Bark

Innocent Vein Of Water

An innocent vein of water
Was born from a small morass
Of high ground grazing – bade to go waltzing –
Rabbit like – onto a slope of meadow grass –
Such an infant trickle
Found in inclined rut – its track
A depression – no more –
To draw it into travelling back

To its ocean of conception
Via stream and river – to deliver
Fresh water for re-cycling – re-vaporizing
Anew – flowing as an adolescent life giver
Once more on borrowed hill –
Boiling from crystal rock and loam –
Bursting through high scree
Effervescing as white water foam

To brighten burn or nant in
Celtic sheep graze – first phase
From spring to pasture – on to rich mud flats –
Refreshing satin grasses growing as graze –
To begin once more
As a constant river giving hope –
Helping new life's sprite
Fight the pagan winter to cope

With long days so bleak
They puzzle a near frozen species –
Being (slow bodied) cold blooded creatures –
Hibernating under convenient bits and pieces
Of slip away dross –
When the balminess of summer's lost
To cooling grey day's –
Cold haze – and a sharpness of frost

So an innocent vein of water –
Born from a small paddy of morass
On high grazing – required again to go waltzing
As Cuniculus on a slope of high meadow grass –
This an infant trickle
Gives home to spiny stickle back
Wagering family future
On this – animated – fickle track

Political Correctness

So I've joined the supporters of political correctness
Since it gave couch potatoes more rights to sue
Because they are the enemy of old fashioned success

Now it's put the idea of hard work under duress
And makes mischievous work for idle hands to do –
So I've joined the supporters of political correctness

When it becomes the nadir of sporting prowess
I will form a blind team of men under four feet two
Because they are the enemy of old fashioned success

As is the public gay display of a male on male caress
Once illegal – now right for people like me and you
So I've joined the supporters of political correctness

Since jobs are no longer awarded to men of finesse
But to supporters of perversity who haven't a clue
Because they are the enemy of old fashioned success

So I'm happy to working harder while being paid less
And contributing to indolence with more than my due
So I've joined the supporters of political correctness
Because they are the enemy of old fashioned success

Mistress Love

How mean was mistress love
When I fell for her with feelings
So genuine – so sincere –
While she returns my adoration
Wrapped in string and paper –
Stamped with 'trademark' sneer –
Labelled to a man of mongrel species –
Made up of ire – cut about
And spread around as bits and pieces

She shows me cruel indifference
In this unequal – femonic affair –
Sore are my wits – my diffidence –
My fears – all gone beyond repair –

How morose was I – my melancholy
De-oxygenated in rejection's gasp –
So tight I could not escape its grasp –
I must breathe out all this hell and folly –
Emphysema and collywobbles –
Cobbling at my last – stitching –
Steadying myself against the outcome
Of this unequal strife – as with a wasp
Set free to sting with trademark sneer
All those so 'genuine' – so 'sincere'
Complements – drowned in nettle beer –
Pinned again and again against my wits –
While I stumble over pieces – of my broken bits

Morphine Patch

My pain is regulated by a morphine patch –
That up to now is much a match
For all the discomfort lurking in my joints
That this naiad Morph – from her stream anoints –
So far this fairy flies for now –
Until she came to rest beneath the bough
And forgot to spread a patch – anew
So pain now like a serpent grew –

With fangs corrupting me – through
Injection – of an obnoxious venom brew

So aided by buprenorphine break through
Tablets – to be taken – one or two
Sublinguals – dissolved beneath the tongue –
To take away that sharpness as though stung
By hornets – just as nortriptyline desensitises –
So mocrogal – dissolved – emphasizes
The need to be intestine blockage free –
That is why these potions all agree
To work in a medicated unity

So we move on to saliveze oral spray
To be used at any time of day –
To lubricate the driest of digestive glands
So sore mouths shape words all can understand –
Can swallowing simvastatin – amlodopine
And senna tablets make one green? –
Clopidogrel – folic acid – sodium docusate
Sound like artefacts archaeologists are required to date –
But however – when prescribed anew –
They – altogether – are my much needed brew
Along with several others too!

Note:
The Author is expressing how miserable it can be when having to spend so much time taking medicines. Though he wishes it known that he feels well treated by the National Health System

Hardly Held At Bay

It is unfortunate that old age and ill health
Came upon me in the way of stealth –
Roughing up my patina of well polished
Youthful vim and vigour – now abolished
By an unholy list of wrongs and ills –
To be challenged by patch and pills
That only chivvy devilment's array
Of dull diseases – hardly held at bay

Shallow defences do little to arrest
This creeping paralysis of viral pests –
Shabby (cancer distorted) corpuscles –
Soar throats – sweats and aching muscles –
Painful lumbar joints and twisted hips –
Saliva starved – dried and split soar lips –
Brings encrusted words without splurches
While uncontrolled in pitch and yawing lurches

In place of well practiced upright balance –
I'm now victim to a (St Vitas) styled dalliance
With the aggravated staggers and jaunty jitters
Bringing need to take chair with forced sitters –
To contemplate on so much lost opportunity
In the way that fate turned on a luckless me –
Yes it's unfortunate the way that stealth
Came upon me – with old age and sickly health

Played By The Keys

A young lady I was most fond of –
Who could coo as good as any turtle dove –
Had just joined the village choir
So I went along – with this girl I most desire –
She seemed quite welcome – I would say
As many members asked her to stay –
But I wasn't at all happy when the choir master
Thanked her for avoidin' a near disaster
At his house – for the previous three weeks –
Where he said she'd expertly
Oiled his pips and his squeaks

I volunteered to be in the choir
But they had all the folk they did require –
So I said I'd be happy to work
For the organist as I'd never been known to shirk –
She said she'd need me for the blowin'
So I took off my coat in order
That I could better prepare for the showin' –
I started a blowin' so fiercely that it
Took me down on my knees –
She said, "You'll do no good a puffin'
'Cos this harmonium's played – by pressing on the keys."

I did my best – the harmonium to pump –
But I only weakened the hose – causing a lump
To swell up in its air pipe – the like
Of which she'd not seen since the last puncture in her bike –
She said I would have to go home with her

Before we could complete any further
Learning – she said I was to be ready
To go down nice and steady –
As though in prayer – onto my knees –
Then open up her love chest
By playing with her willing keys

The Logging Trio

From Millet's Oil Painting 'The wood Sawyers'

Practised journeymen arrive
Somewhere between the hours of four and five
Take off their coats and hats
Pick up the rusted – rested cross-cut – that's
Well greased and newly set –
Keen as they – now all three are met –
To draw the saw across the log
At the mill steeped in heavy mist and fog

The abrading blade cuts deep
Into the log and all who try to sleep –
Her abrasive curses shout
As untuned accompaniment – let out
From hoarse – soar throats –
With a phlegm – of course (oak tree) oats
Falling on foragers (now awake)
Who rake the piling dust for hunger's sake

So this scene is set for a play
Of (such subject matter as) the working day
A cast of moving statue men –
Toing and froing torsos sway again and again –
Blinking eyelid's tears must
Wrap around each crumb of wooden dust –
To drive out ocular irritations
Caught and washed by tear duct irrigations

Axes swing and land alike
As hammers swing – gainst wedge and spike
Bringing blisters to the fore
On hands that flame in pain – each time more
Painful than before – as they saw
Up anew – with this sweat stained handle chore –
For two score or more years
As do Millet's (keen artisan) sawyers and cleavers

Just as damping vapour's cold
Is caught – less by younger – more by old –
Cursing – choking lumberjack –
Splayed of legs – pained of rheumatic back –
Gnarled and bent the old man
Went upon his weary way – but sadly ran
Into a pneumonia germ – that may
Halt his late night quest – for a place to stay

Flesh And Bone

Please don't part me from my nature
From my nature's trends –
If you do – at least give me
A chance to mend –
Don't kick out at me –
Don't shackle me
In the chains of misery

Please recall I am of flesh and bone
So please don't strip me
Of my dignity – if you do
I'll die alone –
Don't mock me –
Don't bind me
In restraints of sanguinity
For my blood – it must flow inside me

Please put me in my place of nature
Introduce me to adventure –
Show me those ways
To satisfy my days –
If not I am unfulfilled –
Not free nor self willed –
But if educated –
In places highly rated –
My nature will at least be sated

Nelson's Dockyard

I saw a girl with long blonde hair
So self possessed it wasn't fair –
I felt the need to speak to her
But was dumb struck by her coat of fur.
Not the fur of which I'd ever write –
But then again – I think I might –
Though it could bring embarrassment –
If remarking on its musky scent

It was of the savage rodent kind
And in it she went around in my mind
Beneath it – what did she wear –
An expensive dress laundered with due care –
Quite stretched Jeans and tight stretched jumper
Or a skimpy dress – known as a little black number –
Clothes that her ripest secrets could express
Such as a red transparent nurses dress.

How I wish she would return
And read her stories of deep concern –
Smile and giggle now and then
To reaffirm that she is back again –
Hearing Marge's voice say, "Lynn
We'll hear your work so please begin" –
She clears her throat and takes me
Cruising – around in the Caribbean sea

Wild Flowers

Walking through the fresh woods in May
And over moors no sound was heard –
St. Patrick's cabbage calling stay
Without a word

To warn MacKay's Horsetail thistle –
Jersey Lily – Lords and Ladybirds –
So Twiggy Mullein's shrill whistle
Needed not a word

As Love-Lies-Bleeding – Devil's Bit
Shaggy soldier – the quite absurd
Ivy Broom and wet cuckoo spit
Want not a word

So as Ladies Mantle or Willow Herb
Will Touch-Me-Not as the buzzard
Falls in Yorkshire Fog – Sweet Alison
Says not a word

All Credit Lost

I was pleased –

They were not –

Thought my work fine –

They did not –

So I became waste
Sent as garbage –
Where I did not belong
Under low wattage –
Abandoned to the shredder
Told by them
I should know better –
Shaken – crushed –
Turned upside down
Reclassified as dust
Windswept – blown
For a generation –
Besmirched –
All credit Lost –
Now all I do
Is count the cost

Daisy Garden Unfinished

The whole plot was overgrown
Self seeded – unweeded –
When inspected by a church official –
Suitably tweeded.
Her report stated 'unacceptably unkempt' –
In a long – drawn out –
Documented – diatribe –
Written with (festering) doubt.

But daisies and Buttercups thrived
On the ground – and around in a mind
Feeling them spread with minimal care –
Through the hands of a blind
Woman – Who touched them gently –
So that she could detect
What glory fate had created –
In this wilding aspect.

On receipt of the reprimand –
Written of course –
With barely cloaked threats
Of resorting to force –
The frail old woman asked the reader
To take pen and write,
"Although I can't see – I feel
You people are provoking a fight".

The old woman continued,
"I may be blind – but I find
There is satisfaction grown in my plot –
Pleasing observers of every kind –
I hear that my plot is described
As unkempt by your critical ogress –
Though I prefer to describe it's state
As work still in progress."

I remain yours – undiminished

Daisy Garden – Unfinished.

Ron's Continuing Ill Health

Dear Sir I feel obliged to write this letter
Just to say my son Ron's no better –
He's believed to have a blockage in his ears
Causing a problem whereby he often mishears –
We took him to an ENT specialist
Who thought that Tom might have a cyst
So has kept him in for observation –
And to allow the specialists time fore re-couperation

I know you might think it seems strange
As we haven't had the full range
Of his other problems solved – still being diagnosed –
Though the paperwork to date is enclosed –
As for the fool who saw him smoking –
Ron slipped into the fire while choking
On a rolled up item causing him stress – more or less
Resulting in Tom's visit to A and E – in much distress

The problems he has had with his learning
Have – for a time – been a mystery concerning
His eyesight which had been blamed –
Before more medical investigations claimed
He has perfect sight for he's been to many classes
With the lens missing from his glasses
His excuse was that they'd been stolen
By the new boy whose nose is now swollen

It was not his eyes – but a problem with his bones –
Confirmed by his osteopath Miss Jones –
Who says, "His walk is what we call a sidle
Never on his toes – so he's what we specialists call – bone idle."
They had listened to all his woes –
Even chemically tested all his clothes –
At least there's been a great improvement in his grammar
Since he was paid well to loose his awful stammer

Although I feel I must say on his behalf –
It was unfair of his class mates to laugh –
When he claimed wrongly – on seeing his uncle outside
That he had come to give Ron a ride –
And those jokes don't help – about Ron's faults
Causing him problems with uniformed adults –
Also he has an unfortunate fixation for nuts and bolts –
Mainly firing them from his home made catapults

I was disappointed with some members of staff –
Who laughed the time he broke his bike in half –
By riding it off a Cotswold stone wall
Though thankfully he received no injuries at all –
He has an unfair reputation for having no nerve
Which I feel he doesn't deserve –
And with all those stories of his arrests I can not agree –
They were mostly uncalled for – as he was quickly set free

Sending him to a special school fills me with alarm –
In such places – I feel he could come to harm –
The report goes on to say he is a ring leader
And I object to him being referred to as a 'mischief breeder'
I can only say that I was relieved at the last PTA
When I heard the Ofsted inspector say –
There was no special school that would
Take on Ron – though they were told that they should –
Even when offered an inducement – it still did no good

Temptation

As good living tames the soul
So indolence may lose life's goal –
Letting in the threat of temptation
And greed – his close relation –
With the Devil – these two
Make work for idle hands to do

No wines to grape – no ships to shape
Which leaves us no way of escape –
No sights to see – no shoes to tree –
Without escape no way to be set free
No ankles to socks or cardboard to box
We find ourselves on slippery rocks

No ticks to tack – chimney's to stack –
Temptation lulls us into sliding back –
No gardens to hoe – nor ox to bow –
Misery comes with a north-easterly blow
No tops to hat – no bricks to bat –
All enthusiasm falls fatefully flat

No streets to light – no ships to right –
So we must stretch to full height
And rescue day from night –
By putting libidinous living to flight
And send temptation and his relation
To hell fire's fierce conflagration –
Without any chance of mitigation

Acquired Furnishings

My favourite chair was my only chair
So I found myself sitting there
One arm was broken
The other a token
Appendage

It was given to me by a local stonemason
His wife also gave me a basin
And a small ash stool
That – as a rule
Had a wedge

To keep it steady and a seat made of reeds
Woven in with coloured beads
A pattern could be seen
In red and green
At the edge

But back to my chair my one and only chair
I often wished was one of a pair
Guests sit on the floor
My seating so poor
Some pledge

Of a chair is not the same as having one there
So I tell visitors it's in for repair
They always sigh audibly
Feeling sorry for me
On the ledge

Of my window sill while my guests each sit
Taking turns then suggesting it –
Should have a new role
To block the hole
In my hedge

Cow And Calf

I 'ad to go to Stratford
On the tractor
Which was where I didn't want to go –
Cos it was mid-January
And there was a foot of snow.

Y' see the gaffer 'ad it in for me
'e'd cut me pay in ''alf
Cos of what 'e said
I'd done – to 'is latest Jersey calf

Well I'd milked the cow
As always – titivated 'er
In small ways –
So she was ready for the show.

But 'er entry was rejected
Cos somebody 'ad objected
To 'er being listed
In the show guide
As a cow an' weaner –
Cos 'er 'effer calf 'ad died

The gaffer said as 'ow
The calf 'ad died
Cos of me a milkin' 'er mother
Twice a day – to which
I felt obliged to say –
"Well at least I tried."

At which remark 'is daughter cried
Cos she'd been out for a ride –
Not that it was the ride
That was the reason that she cried –
It seemed more likely to be me –
A claimin' that I'd tried.

Ancient Markets

Ancient markets –
Perseverance called for –
Achievement more – for
All those with toes
In the water – braving blows
From white water flows –
Of fluid commerce

For me ancient markets –
Closed by decree –
To thwart me – business
Rounded – profit surrounded
Taken – grounded –

No buying or selling –
No profits swelling –
Attainable targets – only
There – in the telling

Detached market spirit borrowed –
Skulls drilled and hollowed
But not returned with marrow –
Not restored by the morrow.

So are markets put to the past
Authority laughs –
Nothing lasts – though
We live on –
Pens of hurdles gone

Gavel silent –
Frozen moment – with
Council's condonment –
Drovers trapped –
Wrapped in
Clinicised condolence

Ancient markets
Achieve no more –
By the pennyweight
By the score

Vestiges Of Warmth

(Over ill prepared dishes) –
Inauspicious wishes are mouthed
We used to call grace –
But very little grace is seen
Around the TV hearth –
Set in bright electric lights and
Only vestiges of warmth

The winter draughts seek out
A let – through the hindrance
Of double glazed windows –
And insulated interference –
Subdued is the cutting draught
Till door or window is breached
And chill is delighted to cause stiff neck –
That had only recently – been leached

They call on their frosted friend
To set a precedent in misery –
By encouraging viral spores
In savage bouts of dysentery –
Influenza Asian and Swine –
Treated with tartarate of lime

Pneumonia and colds
Caught in nasal folds –
Microscopic differences
Not seen – not screened out –
Treated with oil of Wintergreen
Rubbed in to where cold had been
Or – administered in drops
For scything down all viral crops.

So cold – we must chase you –
Turn you into visual form
And send you to the zoo –
Unless we here your promise
Not to turn our poor flesh blue –
Or stuff up our nasal passages
And turn our noses to –
A crimson hue

Desperation

When Pain completely stopped any movement

With my pulse pump failing –
Plagued – agued – ailing –
Topping and tailing
Each laboured breath –
Gasped – hoarsely rasped –
Latched – close coupled –
Held by wheezing clasp
And spittle hasp

While desperation singed my veins
Boiled my brains
And bound my heart in
Padlocked chains –
Down in the joyless alley –
Iron gated –
Where penury lurks
for those berated –
Taking flack
For acts unstated

I had arranged to be – where I waited –
Heart beating fast – fairly skated
Upon the chill – still – blue ice
Of breathless sacrifice –
Formed as intended good advice –
While desperation singed my veins
Boiled my brains
And bound my heart in
Padlocked chains –
Tethering fast my last remains

Canoeing

I can't remember exactly when
But a game band of Campden men
Took on a tough canoeing test –
At which they swore to do their best –
First they must seek advice
So once or twice trips were made to Fladbury –
In the old saddlery – in order to train with the Trains –
Canoeists of Olympic fame

Who were keen to help out –
If the lads put the Trains name about –
For they were training – on the whole –
For a place in the (XXIV) Olympiad – in Seoul –
NB. (24th) Olympiad
They put those men – two by two –
Into a fibre glass – canoe –
But what an awful t'do –
When one of the lads lost his shoe

Next task was to acquire some canoes
Built for crews paired in twos –
Sean said, "Alan in the Legion
Had a canoe that was in the region
Of what was required."
So in he went and soon hired
Alan's boat – which was lent free
Because Sean could only afford a liquid fee

The lads then borrowed another two
Made from fibre glass of a bluish hue
So now they set off for Bidford river –
On so cold a day it caused all to shiver –
Several of the lads bravely tried
But only managed a variety of circular rides –
So much planning had gone wrong –
(Only Phil and Tom still paddled on)

Seamus had arrived a trifle late
So went for coffee – settling by the fire grate –
Trevor joined him for a caffeine draught
Too far away to see what made the others laugh –
As the snow was dusting all
Those intrepid few were heading for a fall –
(As Phil and Tom paddled boldly on)
Another crew capsized – all technique sadly gone

Andy and Graham a stout hearted pair –
Who looked the part as they took care
When getting in to the skittish craft –
Andy for'ud and Graham aft –
Intrepid they were but all wasn't well
It was the line taken – all could tell –
As those men still standing on the bank
Called on providence to offer thanks

For the pair's boat took on a wobble
It seemed the victim of a nautical hobble –
For the more they gripped the more it tipped
Until someone's trousers ripped –
As they closed in on their inevitable fate
Andy reached for the water gate
But inevitably the river won –
(As Phil and Tom still paddled on)

In went Andy striving for the shore –
Andy was in but Graham went in more
Striking out for the bank –
Once ashore he shouted, "I have you to thank."
In the direction of Andy –
Who found a towel – that was very handy –
While ignoring all that was going on
(Including Phil and Tom who were paddling boldly on)

The weeks slipped by under a hazy sky
Different men would take a paddle and try
But spring time quickly elapsed
As each man's effort in his turn collapsed –
So it was the time to call a halt
Agreeing that failure was no-one's fault –
All that was left was to tell Phil and Tom
(Who were still paddling boldly on)

The consensus was “a bridge to far”
For this gallant effort – by those who are
Still spoken of as “valiant men” –
Including two who were never seen again –
Rumour has it Phil is now in Florida
Involved in a canoeing wrangle
And Tom’s been spotted around the Bermuda Triangle –
But come what may – I’ll bet that Tom and Phil –
Those two men of outstanding will –
Are paddling – somewhere –
Out there – still

Delivery Boys

A reverie of delivery boys
Left their laden grocery bikes
Long distribution walks
And El Dorado ice cream trikes –
To answer their Countries call
To take part in a boy’s own adventure
For public schoolboys –
Apprentice tool boys –
Undergraduates – all those indentured

All to form a relationship with Sam Brown
Lee Enfield and Lewis Maxim –
As part of their new lives sunk in the ground –
Their attention drawn east –
Invited to a lunatic feast
Of offal and a flood of
Non-crossmatched young blood –
Devoured by stretches of cannibalistic mud

They to carry on the job of delivery –
Officers with chivalry –
To flounce
Other ranks to trounce with bayonet bullet and gut –
Killing accurately – skilled – cut
Or frenzied – well honed devilish slash –
Before taking a fall in a stilted satanic brawl
Smoke choked – unable to crawl –
British artisans – French citizens –
Canadians – Belgian Sub-Officers –
And Arcadian philosophers –
All de-mobilized by prized
Madness – without recourse to compromise –

A battle no nearer won – at the cost
Of an unknown score of fine delivery boys – forever lost

Passengers And Periwinkles

Passengers and periwinkles
All ply the Cornish gold coast –
Wearing shells or parachutes
Or life preservers
Which ever maybe needed most –
So safety is in abundance
As they come to land near tin mine bay
In a modestly practised sort of way

Let large sea ferries carry
People more and more
Helicopters go from door to door
Around the homeland shore –
For the fishermen can only tarry now –
From stern to bow
Idled by their quotas –
In's and out's – controlled by
Government department rotas

But the periwinkles take
The splash zone and thrive
Upon the springly tide –
Smooth and black and
Eating lichens when the moon
And high tides rise – so we
To them – mere men above the
High line – riding iron transport
But they to us – good food
When they (by us) – are caught

So let the periwinkles live
With their barnacles and limpets –
Scanny and sea anemones
For we are not their enemies –
So do not pollute high tide bay –
Don't over fish or pour old rubbish –
Into the frolicking sea – but encourage all those
Rock pool miracles and periwinkles –
In their bid to stay – polished and black
And eating lichen at the high tide – every day

A Metric Island Rhyme

In that skirling liquid bottle glass
A cruel green – not velvet as is mown grass –
Tumbling – crashing as though bilious
Sputum – from a poor wretch – ill fed –
Ill writ – ill harassed – no bed
To lay and prey better for his head.

This enemy of the island batters
Peaceful sleep – discordancy scatters
Her rain – as if to terrorise
Those unwise enough to compromise
With inclemency – not buttressing
Blocking – sealing – addressing

Such is an attack as ocean's fury brings –
That of a shaman dripping madness
As he claims to mend my spirit's pourings –
Restoring wit to me – gone from sadness –
As he waves away the breaking storm
And then returns to his abstract form.

Now weather or not he healed me
Is covered in damp – steaming – controversy –
As small blooms reach out their stigmas
In hasty need of (anther and filament)
Stamen – pollen ladened for fertilization
To ensure the procreation of another generation

So the Island survives and thrives to bring
About – a full fruit weighted spring
As the poor 'sputum wretch' wretches no more
In bed of feathers – off the floor –
Just as the cruel liquid bottle glass
Skirls no more - subsided – leaving velvet grass
To please our coursing feet

Sea – Time – Eternity

Measure me against the sea
She with all her savagery – foam flashing –
Boiling – unmollified lashing –
Howelling windwardly –
Producing piscean fry yearly –
Nursing cetaceans and Bi-valves
By sevens and twelves –
Regurgitating – beating – dashing –
Sending me crashing

Measure me against time
That mistress of the bell – the chime
Maker of dates – clocks and houses –
Regimenting spouses
Causing some to arrive pre-date
and sending others away late –
Setting life's rate –
Shadowing me merely as bate
To be taken at any time –
Maturely advanced or still in my prime

Measure me against eternity
The mistress of history – of longevity –
Shaper of planets – gaseous – scolding –
Orbits eccentric – though holding
She – fondler of all five oceans –
Brewer of their outrageous commotions
Scowler on the frailty of human emotions –
Caught up in strife – where that 'millisecond
Life's span' – by eternity is reckoned

Let me sit at each one's feast –
As civilized man not savage beast –
Teach caution to those left as orphan –
Little rested – sorely tested - more than
Most that sally – tarry or are tiresome –
Oiled with whale – quenched by rum –
Where green waves misbehave
Pre-trained to enslave
All steppers out of line –
Confining lepers and their swine

So show me growths of stalactites –
Cosmic storms and Northern lights
The sea clad in myrtle green and foaming whites –
A crop of crystal stalagmites
Then measure me against the sea
Regurgitating – beating – massing
On time's escapement – passing
Me out to the Cosmos – child of Eternity

Out Of Hell

I walked along the way to purgatory
Without even a moment's glory –
Wishing all was well
But instead hell
Opened up before me –

I asked the barnyard hen
To cluck and lay an egg again
For I am poorly –
But the hen said look again –
For I can't help you with your glory

I asked the farmyard cat
But she just spat
As she choked upon
A piece of fat –
Blaming me for her
Malady – saying
I should consult the goat

With whom I spoke – just briefly –
The goat said I must find
And tell my true muse –
In order to repel my blues
And keep me out of hell
Bringing me back for a spell
Of good advice and usefulness

Global Holocaust

The Earth's crust erupts
In scalding tantrum throws
Of boiling larva flows –
Belching red hot sputum out
From a pouring crater spout –
Volcanic spoil
Running over fertile soil
Does not amass
As much greenhouse gas –
As the human race –
Not able to keep pace
With man's coal and oil synergy
To sate his cravings for –
(By now) low stocks of finite energy –

Urgency is buried in procrastination
While the G20 nations
Go into collective hibernation –
Sleeping in their CO2 emitting homes
Bought by toxic money loans –
Before waking and leaving –
Heaving in exhaust polluting cars
To expensive restaurants and bars –

All fiddling – Nero like –
While destruction – ground zero like –
Carries on – unabated
Not yet sated –
In global warming ructions –
Head long into the earth's destruction –
Instead of taking time to think
Which could still pull man back –
From the brink – of global holocaust.

Flight Of Friendship

That flitting dragonfly –
Friendship – passed him by –
High above the outreach
Of his clapping hands
Beyond wispy sedges' trapping strands –
To bend beneath
Shadowed rafters of bramble –
As though to escape – his coarse preamble.

There the reacher comes to harm
As he tries to grasp again – friendships arm –
His rapidly rusting hand
Is maimed – stained with scorn –
As though snagged on cruel blackthorn –
Pricked – like conscience was
Said to be –
Leached of good sense –
And dignity – without recall to recompense.

"Where does friendship rest?"
He cries – "Is that flitting pest caressed
Across a troubled breast –
Or squeezed among the senses
Sprawled out laterally or measured – head to toe –
Primed to combat woe –
Maybe Lost –
Or merely tossed away –
As a cipher – gone un-decoded –
Or a ticking bomb – primed – yet unexploded."

Though potentially volatile –
Friendship might hand out comfort with a smile –
To allay mistrust –
Which he may do with truth – or just pretend
To be a friend –
As might his henchmen – grief – and guilt –
Offer their hands (as they would) –
Around the grave of course –
While freshly bleached – of true remorse.

That flitting dragonfly
Friendship – left the Reacher to sigh
Bellow his weeping – outstretched hands –
Wound in wretched bands
And about to be timed out – no doubt –
By the ticking clock of grief – as sorrow and guilt
Bow their heads above a 'friend' –
As they send the Reacher to his end

The seeds of friendship seem to swirl around –
Unbound –
For a while – infuriate –
Then – too quickly – dissipate.

Glories Conquering Way

I once fought for glory
Till glory won the day
And then – when glory
Marched on with a fife
And drum escort – I was
Left behind – to fester –
a castaway

My lucidity of wit
Numbed by the chemicals
I was mixed with each day –
Marched with me – down
Glory's conquering way –
Leaving me behind –
a castaway

Recruited as expendable – a tool
For high church – high society
High opinion – high morality
Nurtured in a Public school –
Highness above a public fool –
a castaway

Limbs lost – lives shortened
Actions delayed – nerves frayed
To little more than a winter's day –
Caught last out – in order of play
Prayers whispered – importuned –
a castaway

So I and glory drift now – apart
He – inept – insensitive –
About affairs of the heart
Or the way we die – the tears
We cry as death comes in grey
As we are left behind to play –
a castaway

Autobiography Of A Cricket Ball

From the umpires pocket out of sight
I make my way into the light –
My new leather coat polished deepish red –
For in the right hands I become an object of some dread
Now put in a hand of ebony
Sinewy fingers – tight grip turns them to mahogany
As I am carried a long way from the wicket
Called to play – is this really what's called cricket

Tossed and caught – momentarily freed
Then I and he set off at speed
I am launched – the bowler is called a quick
I am in flight – feeling sick
I bang into the grassless strip centre field
Bounce and make the batsman yield –
The dogs of war snarling in the slips –
Shout out, "Catch it." as from the bat I seemed to clip –

Then I flew towards the slip at third –
From the slip cordon audible groans were heard
As I was scratched by uncut nails
Then dropped as the third slip fails
To take me clean – so left I am to cover point –
Who picks me up and with his sweat does me anoint
And so polished he hurls me back to a man with curls
Who asks the captain to give him a whirl

I am turned into a projectile again and again –
As bowlers try in vain to brain
The batsman – by propelling me fearfully fast –
They though quickly knock me out – into my past
All polish gone and battered out of shape
Aided by batsmen who launch me over the boundary tape
Where there is a drunken shamble
Of spectators who turn my life into a scramble

If there is another life – I wish to be the one who hurls
And is six foot eight with a mop of long black curls –
So becoming a frightening quick –
Who sends down the ball so fast it makes him sick –
While trying to hit the batsman on the head –
Or failing that – to fill him full of dread –
In fact I don't mind what I come back as – at all
As long as it's not as a clattered Cricket Ball

Note:
Cricket from the point of view of the ball

From The Past

In memory of David Hobbs 1945 – 1973, Leukaemia Victim

A hushed gathering – those who could
Walked to the grave and stood
Bear headed – as they should
While he was lowered
To rest – dressed in polished cedar wood.

There were those ageing stiff old men
Who remembered the time when
He – Oh what was it again.
Can't remember now
Just what it was he had been known for then.

He had died too soon at twenty eight –
On an early to mid-September date
That day we lost a valued mate
Who had not been well –
Finally to fall – to a lingering cancer fate.

If he came back – who would he be?
Children all passed thirty three
And much older now than he –
A returning spirit perhaps –
Come to re-unite his scattering of family.

Would he find it difficult to gauge
Spending credit beyond a wage?
Or control his growing rage
At the disrespect endemic
Among those – of this 'more indifferent age'.

Would anybody stop to hear him yell
That he has old values left to sell?
Would people wish him well?
In this 'more selfish age'
Or would they make his return a living hell?

Olympics

So at last they arrive – with a flood
Of enthusiasm – pressurized blood
Stiffening sinews – media hype
And kilometres of the ciber type –
Capital's games handed out
Given 'peace-meal' no doubt
To lesser venues – a public school –
South Coast water venues – quiet as a rule –
But over whelmed to be let
Promote each sport seen as a water jewel

Olympic celebration which brings
Imbibing of libations under five rings –
Using the sentinel of propriety
To take care of my sobriety –
As I think long of past aspirations
No longer able to raise even palpitations

Realizing most folk have little interest –
Considering them a minorities behest –
After all – people live out their lives
Not knowing of a young boy who dives
Or a Jamaican giant strider –
Or young girl show jumping rider –
Nor the lack of security powerless to arrest
Those foolish pests
Who would mock the games and wreck 'em
While graffitising – David Beckham

Gypsies texting the price of peas
Lightly pollinated by dwindling bees
Year twelves exchanging 4G and 5G deeds –
Complaining about broadband speeds –
The games not cool enough for them
Their sports contain only electronic men

Do the games stand up to reputation
Or should they relent to a headphone deputation
Of ciber relay texters –
Swarming like post-war starlings –
The precious little darlings
Concrete in self belief
Though their wisdom pile is just a heap
So we who enjoy wish them asleep
And let the longman leap –
While medal winners – with emotion weep

Note:
A rustic view of the limitations of the Olympic Games to inspire young people to take up sport

Mail Failed

The moment I read mail failed
My heart sank – complexion paled –
For the importance – in which I held
Such communications – is cut and felled –
Returned marked 'undeliverable page'
Turned my reading to a rage

The 'world wide web' evolved
It's said – as a melting pot
For passing news – while still hot –
In the heads of those involved
With the silicon chip – pouring
Bits and bights of extrapolation
In mega and giga sized storing
Chips – for egregious information

Automatic acknowledgements delay
Travellers through space – on their way –
By light years – extra terrestrially – about
Retrieving these few flash mails – but does 'being out'
Warrant an 'out of office' reply? – to say
"I'm sorry but I'm not here today."

Sacks of ethereal information to unpack –
Repack – and sent back to the in-box –
With warnings of viruses and a lack
Of protection via Google or Firefox –
But my firewall is installed at small cost
Simply in cheap confirmation
Of this continuous flow of mis-information –
So now I say Yahoo to Google
I'm not prepared to pay much more – in being a lot less frugal